"No one can fully understand the meaning of love unless he's owned a dog. He can show you more honest affection with a flick of his tail than a man can gather through a lifetime of handshakes."
—Gene Hill, "The Dog Man" from *Tears & Laughter,* 1981

Love of
Dogs

Todd R. Berger, Editor

Foreword by Roger Caras

Voyageur Press

PetLife
LIBRARY

Compiled and edited by Todd R. Berger
Designed by Kristy Tucker
Printed in Hong Kong

99   00   01   02   03   5   4   3   2   1

Library of Congress Cataloging-in-Publication Data

Love of dogs : the ultimate tribute to our best friend / Todd. R. Berger, editor ; foreword by Roger Caras.
     p.   cm. — (Petlife library)
    ISBN 0-89658-412-7
    1. Dogs—Anecdotes. 2. Dogs—Pictorial works. 3. Dog owners—Anecdotes. I. Berger, Todd R., 1968- . II. Series.
    SF426.2.L69 1999
    636.7—dc21

Distributed in Canada by Raincoast Books, 8680 Cambie Street, Vancouver, B.C. V6P 6M9

Published by Voyageur Press, Inc.
123 North Second Street, P.O. Box 338, Stillwater, MN 55082 U.S.A.
651-430-2210, fax 651-430-2211

Educators, fundraisers, premium and gift buyers, publicists, and marketing managers: Looking for creative products and new sales ideas? Voyageur Press books are available at special discounts when purchased in quantities, and special editions can be created to your specifications. For details contact the marketing department at 800-888-9653.

Permissions
We have made every effort to determine original sources and locate copyright holders of the excerpts in this book. Grateful acknowledgment is made to the writers, publishers, and agencies listed below for permission to reprint material copyrighted or controlled by them. Please bring to our attention any errors of fact, omission, or copyright.
"Dog Training" from *One Man's Meat* by E. B. White. Copyright © 1940 by E. B. White, renewed 1998 by Joel White. Reprinted by permission of Tilbury House, Publishers, Gardiner, Maine.
"The Runt" from *Dumb-Bell of Brookfield* by John Taintor Foote. Copyright © 1946 by John Taintor Foote. Republished in 1993 by The Lyons Press in the collection *Dumb-Bell of Brookfield, Pocono Shot, and Other Great Dog Stories*, edited by Timothy Foote. Reprinted by permission of Timothy Foote.
"Intelligent and Loyal" from *Intelligent and Loyal: A Celebration of the Mongrel* by Jilly Cooper. Copyright © 1981 by Jilly Cooper. Published by Eyre Methuen. Reprinted in English by permission of Random House UK Limited.
"Hermann" from *The Lord God Made Them All* by James Herriot. Copyright © 1981 by James Herriot. Reprinted in the United States by permission of St. Martin's Press Incorporated. Reprinted in all other territories by permission of David Higham Associates for Michael Joseph Limited.
"Moses" by Walter D. Edmonds. Copyright © 1938 by Walter D. Edmonds, renewed 1965 by Walter D. Edmonds. First published in *The Atlantic Monthly*. Reprinted by permission of Harold Ober Associates.

Page 1: *A five-year-old hugs her Komondor, a sheepdog with roots in Hungary.* Photo © Layne Kennedy
Pages 2-3: *The reddish coat of a purebred golden retriever is accentuated by the crimson reflection of a nearby building.* Photo © Lon E. Lauber
Page 3 inset: *Two dogs glide to freedom closely followed by a straggling cohort.* Photo © Layne Kennedy
Page 5: *Two boys fish from a homemade raft with their best friend.* Photo © Dick Dietrich
Page 6: *Mischievous even at the tender age of six (weeks), a dewy-eyed, bewhiskered golden puppy peers around the edge of a shed door.* Photo © William H. Mullins

Contents

Foreword

by Roger Caras

 During the Paleolithic age, approximately 15,000 years ago, our cave-dwelling forebears did something that we still do today. As a matter of fact, it may be just about the only thing not connected to survival and procreation that we share with the early Stone Age people. The cave people began to pet canine companions as a source of joy and comfort. That makes our interaction with our dogs arguably the most natural thing we do, or at least the oldest thing we do outside of the essential biology of being human and the struggle for survival.

Consider this, too. We have five conventional senses: sight, hearing, smell, taste, and touch. For all but a small percentage of us today the sense we rely on least is touch. We are generally unaware that it even exists, this tactile sense, unless we are surgeons or watch repairmen or belong to some other discrete crafts group requiring an exquisite sense of contact. But there are some exceptional circumstances not connected to professional need. Our sense of touch is markedly heightened during contact with our pets. Did you ever try to be close to your dog or even a dog new to you without petting it, making physical contact with it, using your sense of touch?

Expressing love for a human partner, cuddling and stroking a child, touching affectionately your companion animal are not equivalent activities, certainly, but they are things that come from the same corner of the room. We love our dogs and they love us after their own fashion in an ancient and extremely rewarding way.

Pugs likely originated over 2,500 years ago in Buddhist monasteries in Tibet. Modern-day pug lovers relish their affectionate intelligence, though the squished-face little guy will eat you out of house and home if given half a chance. Photo © Henryk T. Kaiser/Transparencies, Inc.

Our languages are deficient when it comes to defining or describing what animals do or feel, and words often fail us, too, when we want to describe our own feelings about animals. It is a relationship that literally defies description.

We know well enough how our dogs make us feel but how do we describe it? Can we describe it? Furthermore, how do we describe or define how animals feel about us? Licking, tail wagging, flopping over, whining and wiggling—are these love manifestations, or simply ways of submitting or ways of begging for food?

Just about the only thing we can rely on is our own experience which we must accept as empirical evidence. My wife and I presently live with eight dogs. In our forty-four years of married life, we have had about fifty dogs. Our son and his family have two dogs, my daughter and her family have four dogs, and we interact with that extended canine family as well. Therein lies a lot of empirical evidence!

Without having very precise language to work with, I would have to say that I *love* my dogs and my dogs *love* me. That is equally true for the rest of the human members of this very actively loving family.

I take great pleasure in knowing intellectually how old this affair between man and dog is, how natural it is to both our species and I know, too, how it makes me feel and obviously makes the dogs of our lives feel. No words for these things exist (*love* is admittedly inadequate), but the feelings, the peace, the warmth, and, at the same time, the rewards and the heart's adventure certainly are there. That is what this remarkable anthology is all about: peace, warmth, reward, and adventures of the heart. In their own way, each of the highly skilled and deeply feeling writers chosen for

Above: *A beagle lounges on the porch.* Photo © Norvia Behling
Facing page: *Cocker spaniel puppies and their golden-haired owner snuggle on a warm summer day.* Photo © Barbara von Hoffmann

the task has used what he or she has somehow learned about man and dog to approach the truth of this relationship. Their tales may lack a few words here and there but do not want for emotions and the unique views that make this fine collection work so well.

Roger Caras is the President of the American Society for the Prevention of Cruelty to Animals and the author of seventy books on animals and the environment.

Introduction

by Todd R. Berger

 Everyone has a dog story, a tale about a favorite canine from somewhere in the past. As Albert Payson Terhune wrote in his story "Some Sunnybank Dogs" from *A Book of Famous Dogs*, "Soon or late, every dog's master's memory becomes a graveyard; peopled by wistful little furry ghosts that creep back unbidden, at times, to a semblance of their olden lives." Terhune's thought is both depressing and uplifting, but either way rings true. Wherever we go on this earth, whatever occupies our time, that collection of furry ghosts is right by our side, occasionally rising from eternity and causing us to smile broadly. A dog story is a part of us, a happy bookmark in time.

I have my own ghosts. There was Jenny, a beagle, normally high-spirited and capable of the heartiest of yowls. She would go absolutely nuts when you reached down to give her a good rub, rolling on her back to allow aggressive scratching of her chest. She was a beautiful, inherently lovable family hound of the highest order. But when you called her, she just looked at you. Wouldn't budge at all.

"Come on, Jenny," I said. "*Come*, Jenny!" a little louder, harder. She sat there, tilting her head slightly, looking at me. She really had no idea what I wanted, no idea what she was supposed to do. She was a little daft.

I certainly don't mean to imply beagles are inherently stupid. In fact, they are, in general, known for their intelligence. Jenny's dimness was certainly an anomaly, and directly traceable to a veterinary mishap ten years earlier. She had had a massive allergic reaction to a rabies inoculation and, well, "died." Some frantic veterinary action restarted her heart, but the minute or so without circulation left Jenny a tad slow.

The Chihuahua, sometimes weighing as little as two pounds (0.91 kg), is the world's smallest dog.
Photo © Alan and Sandy Carey

A papillon puppy surprises a youngster of another species. Photo © Norvia Behling

"From behind a wooden crate we saw a long black muzzled nose
poking round at us. We took him out—soft, wobbly, tearful; set him down on his four,
as yet not quite simultaneous legs, and regarded him.
He wandered a little round our legs, neither wagging his tail nor licking at our hands;
then he looked up, and my companion said: 'He's an angel!'"
—John Galsworthy, "Memories" from The Inn of Tranquility, *1912*

"Come *on*, Jenny!"

Hopeless. I walked over, picked her up, and carried her into the house. Jenny was pretty dumb, but when I was a boy she was my best friend.

Then there was Susan, an independent-minded, slightly brilliant shorthaired miniature dachshund with a haughty attitude and a mouth like a Hoover. It was excellent advice to not reach for that chunk of beef roast that slipped off your fork onto the carpet, unless you were living a life of crime and wanted to lose your fingerprints. She pretty much ran the place and preferred that the people who happened to be about keep out of her way.

One day Dad brought home a new puppy to join our household, which was already populated by a cat named Barney, two or three goldfish, the parakeets Steve and Pete, and Susan. The puppy, a German shepherd soon to be named Taj, after some extended explorations and a pee in the backyard, attempted to make friends with the elongated hound, which was much smaller than the new pup. Susan immediately bit the shepherd square on the nose, Taj letting out a *yowlp* that echoed through the ages. Even years later, when full grown and perhaps ten times the weight of the wiener dog, Taj gave Susan a wide berth.

And then there was Johann, another shepherd and a huge, bearlike dog that tipped the scales at some 150 pounds (68 kg). His tremendous snout and powerful body made him an excellent companion for a late-night stroll through the nearby city park; the intimidating presence of such a king-size German shepherd made any would-be marauders with malicious intent think twice before approaching the dog-walker.

Fitting comfortably in a handbag, a furry-faced little dog hits the road with its owner. Photo © Mike Booher/Transparencies, Inc.

But despite his size and the fear he often instilled in the uninitiated, Johann was anything but fierce and dangerous. He was as mellow as a Sunday, as comfortable as flannel pajamas. A great, big sweatheart of a dog that loved to put his massive head in your lap and let you mess with his ears. His barrel of a body was huggable, and his cavernous yawns were contagious. His spirit is still with me when times get too fast.

All dog lovers like a good story about a canine. Some of us are especially gifted at telling dog stories, and so one day such storytellers pick up a pen and write them down. Dog stories have become a genre of fiction of

its own due to great writers such as James Herriot, E. B. White, and others. As we read these tales of the masters, it is easy to substitute subconsciously our own Rover from our childhood for Albert Payson Terhune's Lad or Walter Edmonds's Moses. Reading a dog story by a talented writer is as comfortable and natural as rubbing the ears of a German shepherd while his big ol' head rests in your lap. It just plain feels good.

Like a good story, beautiful canine photographs and works of art trigger a flood of memories. The antics recorded by the world's best seem so much like the antics of a dog in our past, our very own Lab, Airedale, poodle, or schnauzer. We look at a gorgeous photograph and say something like, "Oh! Remember how Hortense used to keep tennis balls in her jowls just like that!" to all within earshot—a comment amusing to all except the tennis players. The photographs, like memories of a slightly daft beagle or a cocky dachshund, are comfortable, too. We've been here before, and it just plain feels good.

About *Love of Dogs*

So now we come to this book, a collection of great dog writing, beautiful dog photographs and paintings. No, you won't see a photograph of your childhood dog Snidely, or Princess, or Bob, but you will see photographs that kind of look like that dog ghost of yours, and the memories will come streaming back. You won't read a story about your dog Amos, or Samson, or Ruthie, but some of the things that Dumb-Bell, or Lad, or Moses do will ring so true, be so universally doglike, that the actual main character doesn't matter so much as do the thoughts and conversations that ensue after you set the book down. If this book had fur, you'd undoubtedly pet it.

So, snuggle up in a favorite chair—with a wonderful hound close at hand—and take a trip down memory lane with *Love of Dogs*.

A Jack Russell terrier bravely confronts and attempts to stare down a lop-eared rabbit. Photo © Alan and Sandy Carey

"A dog, more than any other creature,
it seems to me, gets interested in one subject, theme,
or object, in life, and pursues it with a fixity of purpose which would
be inspiring to Man if it weren't so troublesome."
—E. B. White, "A Boston Terrier"
from One Man's Meat, *1939*

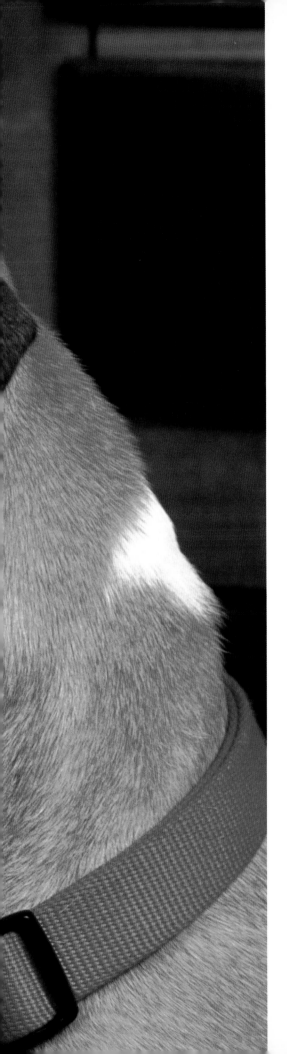

PART I

Love of Dogs

"He cannot be a gentleman that loveth not a dog."
—Proverb

Above: *A Massachusetts state police officer takes a moment to praise his drug-sniffing German shepherd partner.* Photo courtesy UPI/Corbis–Bettman
Left: *A jowly profile from an otherwise quite lovable bulldog.* Photo © Norvia Behling

The Coming of Lad

by Albert Payson Terhune

 Some might argue that the bond between dog and owner is stronger than most human relationships, that the eternal loyalty, sloppy enthusiasm at first sight, and awkward foibles make a dog seem close to the ideal human friend—a trusted, non-judgmental, imperfect being that is just plain happy to see you. Love for such a beast seems only natural.

Albert Payson Terhune published his first book, *Syria from the Saddle,* a travelogue of a post-graduate horseback tour, in 1896, and worked for many years at the *New York Evening World* as a reporter and editor. But, as he said later, this was work that he "loathed," and it was through dog stories that Terhune eventually found the freedom and satisfaction he craved.

He published his first dog story, "His Mate," in *Redbook* in 1915, and the phenomenal success of his dog writing led him to quit his newspaper job a year later. His first book-length piece about a canine, the bestselling *Lad: A Dog,* came out in 1919, and Terhune never looked back. He wrote some sixty books and countless short stories, nearly all of which featured a dog.

"The Coming of Lad," from *The Heart of a Dog,* published in 1924, spotlights Terhune's popular collie in his earliest days with the family. But even at a young age, the playful Lad saves the day in a most miraculous way.

Rough collies originated in Iceland, but their name is Scottish in origin, a moniker adapted from "colley," a name for certain types of sheep. Queen Victoria kept a rough collie at her Scottish estate. Photo © Alan and Sandy Carey

IN THE MILE-AWAY village of Hampton, there had been a veritable epidemic of burglaries—ranging from the theft of a brand-new ash-can from the steps of the Methodist chapel to the ravaging of Mrs. Blauvelt's whole lineful of clothes, on a washday dusk.

Up the Valley and down it, from Tuxedo to Ridgewood, there had been a half-score robberies of a very different order—depredations wrought, manifestly, by professionals; thieves whose motor cars served the twentieth century purpose of such historic steeds as Dick Turpin's Black Bess and Jack Shepard's Ranter. These thefts were in the line of jewelry and the like; and were as daringly wrought as were the modest local operators' raids on ash-can and laundry.

It is the easiest thing in the world to stir humankind's ever-tense burglar-nerves into hysterical jangling. In house after house, for miles of the peaceful North Jersey region, old pistols were cleaned and loaded; window fastenings and door-locks were inspected and new hiding-places found for portable family treasures.

Across the lake from the village, and down the Valley from a dozen country homes, seeped the tide of precautions. And it swirled at last around the Place—a thirty-acre homestead, isolated and sweet, whose grounds ran from highway to lake; and whose wisteria-clad gray house drowsed among big oaks midway between road and water; a furlong or more distant from either.

The Place's family dog—a pointer—had died, rich in years and honour. And the new peril of burglary made it highly needful to choose a successor for him.

The Master talked of buying a whalebone-and-steel-and-snow bull terrier, or a more formidable if more greedy Great Dane. But the Mistress wanted a collie. So they compromised by getting the collie.

He reached the Place in a crampy and smelly crate; preceded by a long envelope containing an intricate and imposing pedigree. The burglary-preventing problem seemed solved.

But when the crate was opened and its occupant stepped gravely forth, on the Place's veranda, the problem was revived.

All the Master and the Mistress had known about the newcomer—apart from his price and his lofty lineage—was that his breeder had named him "Lad."

From these meagre facts they had somehow built up a picture of a huge and grimly ferocious animal that should be a terror to all intruders and that might in time be induced to make friends with the Place's vouched-for occupants. In view of this, they had had a stout kennel made and to it they had affixed with double staples a chain strong enough to restrain a bull.

(It may as well be said here that never in all the sixteen years of his beautiful life did Lad occupy that or any other kennel nor wear that or any other chain.)

Even the crate which brought the new dog to the Place failed somehow to destroy the illusion of size and fierceness. But, the

A black Lab shakes water every which way while practicing retrieving on a late-autumn day. Photo © Bill Buckley/
The Green Agency

"One evening as he was walking by the river and quietly staring into the water, it suddenly seemed to him as though something were floundering in the ooze close to the bank. He bent down and, behold, a small puppy, white with black spots, which, despite all its endeavours, utterly unable to crawl out of the water, was struggling, slipping, and quivering all over its wet, gaunt little body. Gerásim gazed at the unfortunate puppy, picked it up with one hand, thrust it into his breast, and set out with great strides homeward."—Ivan Turgeniev, *"Mumú" from* The Novels and Stories of Ivan Turgenieff, *1903*

moment the crate was opened the delusion was wrecked by Lad himself.

Out on to the porch he walked. The ramshackle crate behind him had a ridiculous air of a chrysalis from which some bright thing had departed. For a shaft of sunlight was shimmering athwart the veranda floor. And into the middle of the warm bar of radiance Laddie stepped—and stood.

His fluffy puppy-coat of wavy mahogany-and-white caught a million sunbeams, reflecting them back in tawny-orange glints and in a dazzle of snow. His forepaws were absurdly small, even for a puppy's. Above them the ridging of the stocky legbones gave as clear promise of mighty size and strength as did the amazingly deep little chest and square shoulders.

Here one day would stand a giant among dogs, powerful as a timber-wolf, lithe as a cat, as dangerous to foes as an angry tiger; a dog without fear or treachery; a dog of uncanny brain and great lovingly loyal heart and, withal, a dancing sense of fun. A dog with a soul.

All this, any canine physiologist might have read from the compact frame, the proud head-carriage, the smoulder in the deep-set sorrowful dark eyes. To the casual observer, he was but a beautiful and appealing and wonderfully cuddleable bunch of puppyhood.

Lad's dark eyes swept the porch, the soft swelling green of the lawn, the flash of fire-blue lake among the trees below. Then, he deigned to look at the group of humans at one side of him. Gravely, impersonally, he surveyed them; not at all cowed or strange in his new surroundings; courteously inquisitive as to the twist of luck that had set him down here and as to the people who, presumably, were to be his future companions.

Perhaps the stout little heart quivered just a bit, if memory went back to his home kennel and to the rowdy throng of brothers and sisters and, most of all, to the soft furry mother against whose side he had nestled every night since he was born. But if so, Lad was too valiant to show homesickness by so much as a whimper. And, assuredly, this House of Peace was infinitely better than the miserable crate wherein he had spent twenty horrible and jouncing and smelly and noisy hours.

From one to another of the group strayed the level sorrowful gaze. After the swift inspection, Laddie's eyes rested again on the Mistress. For an instant, he stood, looking at her, in that mildly polite curiosity which held no hint of personal interest.

Then, all at once, his plumy tail began to wave. Into his sad eyes sprang a flicker of warm friendliness. Unbidden—oblivious of every one else—he trotted across to where the Mistress sat. He put one tiny white paw in her lap; and stood thus, looking up lovingly into her face, tail away, eyes shining.

"There's no question whose dog he's going to be," laughed the Master. "He's elected you—by acclamation."

Facing page: *A patient terrier waits for its owner to return.* Photo © J. Faircloth/Transparencies, Inc.

The placid but independent nature—along with the Eeyore-like droopy face and ears—have made the basset hound a favorite family pet. Photo © Keith Baum

"Any man with money to make the purchase can become a dog's owner.
*But no man—spend he ever so much coin and food and tact in the effort—may become
a dog's* Master *without the consent of the dog. Do you get the difference? And he whom a dog once
unreservedly accepts as Master is forever that dog's God."*
—*Albert Payson Terhune,* Lad: A Dog, *1919*

The Mistress caught up into her arms the half-grown youngster, petting his silken head, running her white fingers through his shining mahogany coat; making crooning little friendly noises to him. Lad forgot he was a dignified and stately pocket-edition of a collie. Under this spell, he changed in a second to an excessively loving and nestling and adoring puppy.

"Just the same," interposed the Master, "we've been stung. I wanted a dog to guard the Place and to be a menace to burglars and all that sort of thing. And they've sent us a Teddy Bear. I think I'll ship him back and get a grown one. What sort of use is—?"

"He is going to be all those things," eagerly prophesied the Mistress. "And a hundred more. See how he loves to have me pet him! And—look—he's learned, already, to shake hands, and—"

"Fine!" applauded the Master. "So when it comes our turn to be visited by this motor-Raffles, the puppy will shake hands with him, and register love of petting; and the burly marauder will be so touched by Lad's friendliness that he'll not only spare our house but lead an upright life ever after. I—"

"Don't send him back!" she pleaded. "He'll grow up, soon, and—"

"And if only the courteous burglars will wait till he's a couple of years old," suggested the Master, "he—"

Set gently on the floor by the Mistress, Laddie had crossed to where the Master stood. The man, glancing down, met the puppy's gaze. For an instant he scowled at the miniature watchdog, so ludicrously different from the ferocious brute he had expected. Then—for some queer reason—he stooped and ran his hand roughly over the tawny coat, letting it rest at last on the shapely head that did not flinch or wriggle at his touch.

"All right," he decreed. "Let him stay. He'll be an amusing pet for you, anyhow. And his eye has the true thoroughbred expression—'the look of eagles.' He may amount to something after all. Let him stay. We'll take a chance on burglars."

So it was that Lad came to the Place. So it was that he demanded and received due welcome—which was ever Lad's way. The Master had been right about the pup's proving "an amusing pet," for the Mistress. From that first hour, Lad was never willingly out of her sight. He had adopted her. The Master, too—in only a little lesser wholeheartedness—he adopted. Toward the rest of the world, from the first, he was friendly but more or less indifferent.

Almost at once, his owners noted an odd trait in the dog's nature. He would of course get into any or all of the thousand mischief-scrapes which are the heritage of puppies. But, a single reproof was enough to cure him forever of the particular form of mischief which had just been chidden. He was one of those rare dogs that learn the Law by instinct; and that remember for all time a command or a prohibition once given them.

For example: On his second day at the Place, he made a furious rush at a neurotic mother hen and her golden convoy of chicks. The Mistress—luckily for all concerned—was within call. At her sharp summons the puppy wheeled, midway in his charge, and trotted back to her. Severely, yet trying not to laugh at his worried aspect, she scolded Lad for his misdeed.

An hour later, as Lad was scampering ahead of her, past the stables, they rounded a corner and came flush upon the same nerve-wrecked hen and her brood. Lad halted in his scamper, with a suddenness that made him skid. Then, walking as though on eggs, he made an idiotically wide circle about the feathered dam and her silly chicks. Never thereafter did he assail any of the Place's fowls.

It was the same, when he sprang up merrily at a line of laundry, flapping in alluring invitation from the drying ground lines. A single word of rebuke—and thenceforth the family wash was safe from him.

And so on with the myriad perplexing "Don'ts" which spatter the career of a fun-loving collie pup. Versed in the patience-fraying ways of pups in general, the Mistress and the Master marvelled and bragged and praised.

All day and every day, life was a delight to the little dog. He had friends everywhere, willing to romp with him. He had squirrels to chase, among the oaks. He had the lake to splash ecstatically in. He had all he wanted to eat; and he had all the petting his hungry little heart could crave.

He was even allowed, with certain restrictions, to come into the mysterious house itself. Nor, after one defiant bark at a leopardskin rug, did he molest anything therein. In the house, too, he found a genuine cave—a wonderful place to lie and watch the world at large, and to stay cool in and to pretend he was a wolf. The cave was the deep space

beneath the piano in the music room. It seemed to have a peculiar charm to Lad. To the end of his days, by the way, this cave was his chosen resting place. Nor, in his lifetime did any other dog set foot therein.

So much for "all day and every day." But the nights were different.

Lad hated the nights. In the first place, everybody went to bed and left him alone. In the second, his hardhearted owners made him sleep on a fluffy rug in a corner of the veranda instead of in his delectable piano-cave. Moreover, there was no food at night. And there was nobody to play with or to go for walks with or to listen to. There was nothing but gloom and silence and dulness.

"Happiness is a warm puppy."
—Charles Schultz. Photo © Henry H. Holdsworth/Wild by Nature

When a puppy takes fifty cat-naps in the course of the day, he cannot always be expected to sleep the night through. It is too much to ask. And Lad's waking hours at night were times of desolation and of utter boredom. True, he might have consoled himself, as does many a lesser pup, with voicing his woes in a series of melancholy howls. That, in time, would have drawn plenty of human attention to the lonely youngster; even if the attention were not wholly flattering.

But Lad did not belong to the howling type. When he was unhappy, he waxed silence. And his sorrowful eyes took on a deeper woe. By the way, if there is anything more sorrowful than the eyes of a collie pup that has never known sorrow, I have yet to see it.

No, Lad could not howl. And he could not hunt for squirrels. For these enemies of his were not content with the unsportsmanliness of climbing out of his reach in the daytime, when he chased them; but they added to their sins by joining the rest of the world—except Lad— in sleeping all night. Even the lake that was so friendly by day was a chilly and forbidding playfellow on the cool North Jersey nights.

There was nothing for a poor lonely pup to do but stretch out on his rug and stare in unhappy silence up the driveway in the impossible hope that some one might happen along through the darkness to play with him.

At such an hour and in such lonesomeness, Lad would gladly have tossed aside all prejudices of caste—and all his natural dislikes—and would have frolicked in mad joy with the veriest stranger. Anything was better than this drear solitude throughout the million hours before the first of the maids should be stirring or the first of the farmhands report for work. Yes, night was a disgusting time; and it had not one single redeeming trait for the puppy.

Lad was not even consoled by the knowledge that he was guarding the slumbrous house. He was not guarding it. He had not the very remotest idea what it meant to be a watchdog. In all his five months he had never dreamed that there is unfriendliness in the world; or that there is anything to guard a house against.

True, it was instinctive with him to bark when people came down the drive, or appeared at the gates without warning. But more than once the Master had bidden him be silent when a rackety puppy salvo of barking had broken in on the arrival of some guest. And Lad was still in perplexed doubt as to whether barking was something forbidden or merely limited.

"A watchdog is a dog kept to guard the house, usually by sleeping where a burglar would awaken the household by falling over him."— *Anonymous.* Photo © Bill Buckley/The Green Agency

The serene Labrador retriever has an unflappable, loyal personality. Photo © Jack Macfarlane

High-stepping through the snow, a cowboy saddles up and heads out with his dog close behind. Photo © Marilyn "Angel" Wynn

One night—a solemn, black, breathless August night, when half-visible heat lightning turned the murk of the western horizon to pulses of dirty sulphur—Lad awoke from a fitful dream of chasing squirrels which had never learned to climb.

He sat up on his rug, blinking around through the gloom in the half hope that some of those non-climbing squirrels might still be in sight. As they were not, he sighed unhappily and prepared to lay his classic young head back again on the rug for another spell of night-shortening sleep.

But, before his head could touch the rug, he reared it and half of his small body from the floor and focused his nearsighted eyes on the driveway. At the same time, his tail began to wag a thumping welcome.

Now, by day, a dog cannot see so far nor so clearly as can a human. But by night—for comparatively short distances— he can see much better than can his master. By day or by darkness, his keen hearing and keener scent make up for all defects of eyesight.

And now three of Lad's senses told him he was no longer alone in his tedious vigil. Down the drive, moving with amusing slowness and silence, a man was coming. He was on foot. And he was fairly well dressed. Dogs— the foremost snobs in creation— are quick to note the difference between a well-clad and a dis- reputable stranger.

Here unquestionably was a visitor:—some such man as so often came to the Place and paid such flattering attention to the puppy. No longer need Lad be bored by the solitude of this particular night. Some one was coming towards the house and carrying a small bag under his arm. Some one to make friends with. Lad was very happy.

Deep in his throat a welcoming bark was born. But he stilled it. Once, when he had barked at the approach of a stranger, the stranger had gone away. If this stranger were to go away, all the night's fun would go with him. Also, no later than yesterday, the Master had scolded Lad for barking at a man who had called. Wherefore the dog held his peace.

Getting to his feet and stretching himself, fore and aft, in true collie fashion, the pup gambolled up the drive to meet the visitor.

The man was feeling his way through the pitch darkness, groping cautiously; halting once or twice for a smoulder of lightning to silhouette the house he was nearing. In a wooded lane, a quarter mile away, his lightless motor car waited.

Lad trotted up to him, the tiny white feet noiseless in the soft dust of the drive. The man did not see him, but passed so close to the dog's hospitably upthrust nose that he all but touched it.

Only slightly rebuffed at such chill lack of cordiality, Lad fell in behind him, tail away, and followed him to the porch. When the guest should ring the bell, the Master or one of the maids would come to the door. There would be lights and talk; and perhaps Laddie himself might be allowed to slip in to his beloved cave.

But the man did not ring. He did not stop at the door at all. On tiptoe he skirted the veranda to the old-fashioned bay windows at the south side of the living room—windows with catches as old-fashioned and as simple to open as themselves.

Lad padded along, a pace or so to the rear—still hopeful of being petted or perhaps even romped with. The man gave a faint but promising sign of intent to romp, by swinging his small and very shiny brown bag to and fro as he walked. Thus ever did the Master swing Lad's precious canton flannel doll before throwing it for him to retrieve. Lad made a tentative snap at the bag, his tail wagging harder than ever. But he missed it. And, in another moment the man stopped swinging the bag and tucked it under his arm again as he began to fumble with a bit of steel.

There was the very faintest of clicks. Then, noiselessly the window slid upward. A second fumbling sent the wooden inside shutters ajar. The man worked with no uncertainty. Ever since his visit to the Place, a week earlier, behind the aegis of a big and bright and newly forged telephone-inspector badge, he had carried in his trained memory the location of windows and of obstructing furniture and of the primitive small safe in the living room wall, with its pitifully pickable lock—the safe wherein the Place's few bits of valuable jewelry and other compact treasures reposed at night.

Lad was tempted to follow the creeping body and the fascinatingly

Miniature schnauzers dressed like jesters of the court on a winter afternoon. Photo © Alan and Sandy Carey

Sled dogs ply their trade along Minnesota's Gunflint Trail, near the Canadian border. Photo © Layne Kennedy

"Instantly all the huskies break into such a chorus of barking and howling that one can scarcely make himself heard. It takes stout ropes and deeply driven stakes to hold the anxious dogs from dashing off helter-skelter today. The anchor ropes are jerked loose, the men holding the dogs leap back. No command is needed, for with one jump the dogs are away, snow flying in clouds from their racing feet."
—John S. O'Brien, By Dog Sled for Byrd, *1931*

Above: *Pointy-eared Norwich terriers are one of the smallest of the terriers.* Photo © Kent and Donna Dannen
Facing page: *The Chesapeake Bay retriever is a favorite among American waterfowlers.* Photo © Gary Kramer

swinging bag indoors. But his one effort to enter the house—with muddy paws—by way of an open window, had been rebuked by the Lawgivers. He had been led to understand that really well-bred little dogs come in by way of the door; and then only on permission.

So he waited, doubtfully, at the veranda edge; in the hope that his new friend might reappear or that the Master might perhaps want to show off his pup to the caller, as so often the Master was wont to do.

Head cocked to one side, tulip ears alert, Laddie stood listening. To the keenest human ears the thief's soft progress across the wide living room to the wall-safe would have been all but inaudible. But Lad could follow every phase of it—the cautious skirting of each chair; the hesitant pause as a bit of ancient furniture creaked; the halt in front of the safe; the queer grinding noise, muffled but persevering, at the lock; then the faint creak of the swinging iron door, and the deft groping of fingers.

Soon, the man started back toward the paler oblong of gloom, which marked the window's outlines from the surrounding black. Lad's tail began to wag again. Apparently, this eccentric person was coming out, after all, to keep him company. Now, the man was kneeling on the window-seat. Now, in gingerly fashion, he reached forward and set the small bag down on the veranda; before negotiating the climb across the broad seat—a climb that might well call for the use of both his hands.

Lad was entranced. Here was a game he understood. Thus, more

than once, had the Mistress tossed out to him his flannel doll, as he had stood in pathetic invitation on the porch, looking in at her as she read or talked. She had laughed at his wild tossings and other maltreatments of the limp doll. He had felt he was scoring a real hit. And this hit he decided to repeat.

Snatching up the swollen little satchel, almost before it left the hand, Lad shook it, joyously, revelling in the faint clink and jingle of the contents. He backed playfully away; the bag-handle swinging in his jaws. Crouching low, he wagged his tail in ardent invitation to the stranger to chase him and to get back the satchel. Thus did the Master romp with Lad when the flannel doll was the prize of their game. And Lad loved such races.

Yes, the stranger was accepting the invitation. The moment he had crawled out on the veranda he reached down for the bag. As it was not where he thought he had left it, he swung his groping hand forward in a half-circle, his fingers sweeping the floor.

Make that enticing motion, directly in front of a playful collie pup—especially if he has something he doesn't want you to take from him—and watch the effect.

Instantly, Lad was athrill with the spirit of the game. In one scurrying backward jump, he was off the veranda and on the lawn, tail vibrating, eyes dancing; satchel held tantalisingly towards its would-be possessor.

The light sound of his body touching ground reached the man. Reasoning that the sweep of his own arm had somehow knocked the bag off the porch, he ventured off the edge of the veranda and flashed a swathed ray of his pocket light along the ground in search of it.

The flashlight's lens was cleverly muffled; in a way to give forth but a single subdued finger of illumination. That one brief glimmer was enough to show the thief a right impossible sight. The glow struck answering lights from the polished sides of the brown bag. The bag was hanging in air some six inches above the grass and perhaps five feet away from him. Then he saw it swing frivolously to one side and vanish in the night.

The astonished man had seen more. Feeble was the flashlight's shrouded rag—too feeble to outline against the night the small dark body behind the shining brown bag. But that same ray caught and reflected back to the incredulous beholder two

Despite shaggy coats that hang down over their eyes, Old English sheepdogs have no problem keeping a wary eye on the flock. Photo © Tara Darling

A toy poodle, with a condescending expression on its face, evaluates a curious Siamese kitten. Photo © Alan and Sandy Carey

"For a man living alone
dogs are almost more important than human beings."
—*Richard Katz,* Solitary Life, *1958*

American foxhounds pursue their quarry led by their master in traditional fox-hunting attire. Photo © Tara Darling

splashes of pale fire—glints from a pair of deep-set collie-eyes.

As the bag disappeared, the eerie fire-points were gone. The thief all but dropped his flashlight. He gaped in nervous dread; and sought vainly to account for the witchwork he had witnessed.

He had plenty of nerve. He had plenty of experience along his chosen line of endeavour. But while a crook may control his nerve, he cannot make it phlegmatic or steady. Always, he must be conscious of holding it in check, as a clever driver checks and steadies and keeps in subjection a plunging horse. Let the vigilance slacken, and there is a runaway.

Now this particular marauder had long ago keyed his nerve to the chance of interruption from some gun-brandishing house-holder; and to the possible pursuit of police; and to the need of fighting or of fleeing. But all his preparations had not taken into account this newest emergency. He had not steeled himself to watch unmoved the gliding away of a treasure-satchel, apparently moving of its own will; nor the shimmer of two greenish sparks in the air just above it. And, for an instant, the man had to battle against a craven desire to bolt.

Lad, meanwhile, was having a beautiful time. Sincerely, he appreciated the playful grab his nocturnal friend had made in his general direction. Lad had countered this, by frisking away for another five or six feet, and then wheeling about to face once more his playfellow and to await the next move in the blithe gambol. The pup could see tolerably well, in the darkness— quite well enough to play the game his guest had devised. And of course, he had no way of knowing that the man could not see equally well.

Shaking off his momentary terror, the thief once more

What dogs find edible will often make their more choosy owners' stomachs turn. Photo © Bill Buckley/The Green Agency

> *"I'm a lean dog, a keen dog, a wild dog, and lone;*
> *I'm a rough dog, a tough dog, hunting on my own;*
> *I'm a bad dog, a mad dog, teasing silly sheep;*
> *I love to sit and bay at the moon, to keep fat souls from sleep."*
> *—Irene McLeod, "Lone Dog" from*
> Songs to Save a Soul, *1915*

pressed the button of his flashlight; swinging the torch in a swift
semicircle and extinguishing it at once; lest the dim glow be seen by
any wakeful member of the family.

That one quick sweep revealed to his gaze the shiny brown bag a
half-dozen feet ahead of him, still swinging several inches above
ground. He flung himself forward at it; refusing to believe he also saw
that queer double glow of pale light, just above. He dived for the
satchel with the speed and the accuracy of a football tackle. And that
was all the good it did him.

Perhaps there is something in nature more agile and dismayingly
elusive than a romping young collie. But that "something" is not a
mortal man. As the thief sprang, Lad sprang in unison with him; darting
to the left and a yard or so backward. He came to an expectant standstill once more; his tail wildly vibrating, his entire furry body tingling
with the glad excitement of the game. This sportive visitor of his was a
veritable godsend. If only he could be coaxed into coming to play with
him every night—!

But presently he noted that the other seemed to have wearied of
the game. After plunging through the air and landing on all fours with
his grasping hands closing on nothingness, the man had remained thus,
as if dazed, for a second or so. Then he had felt the ground all about
him. Then, bewildered, he had scrambled to his feet. Now he was
standing, moveless, his lips working.

Yes, he seemed to be tired of the lovely game—and just when
Laddie was beginning to enter into the full spirit of it. Once in a while,
the Mistress or the Master stopped playing, during the romps with the
flannel doll. And Laddie had long since hit on a trick for reviving their
interest. He employed this ruse now.

As the man stood, puzzled and scared, something brushed very
lightly—even coquettishly—against his knuckles. He started in nervous
fright. An instant later, the same thing brushed his knuckles again, this
time more insistently. The man, in a spurt of fear-driven rage, grabbed
at the invisible object. His fingers slipped along the smooth sides of the
bewitched bag that Lad was shoving invitingly at him.

Brief as was the contact, it was long enough for the thief's sensitive
finger tips to recognise what they touched. And both hands were
brought suddenly into play, in a mad snatch for the prize. The ten avid
fingers missed the bag; and came together with clawing force. But,
before they met, the finger tips of the left hand telegraphed to the
man's brain that they had had momentary light experience with
something hairy and warm—something that had slipped, eel-like, past
them into the night—something that most assuredly was no satchel,
but *alive!*

The man's throat contracted, in gagging fright. And, as before, fear
scourged him to feverish rage.

Recklessly he pressed the flashlight's button; and swung the
muffled bar of light in every direction. In his other hand he levelled the

The simple elegance of a Weimaraner on a South Carolina beach. Photo © J. Faircloth/Transparencies, Inc.

pistol he had drawn. This time the shaded ray revealed to him not only his bag, but—vaguely—the Thing that held it.

He could not make out what manner of creature it was which gripped the satchel's handle and whose eyes pulsed back greenish flares into the torch's dim glow. But it was an animal of some kind—distorted and formless in the wavering finger of blunted light, but still an animal. Not a ghost.

And fear departed. The intruder feared nothing mortal. The mystery in part explained, he did not bother to puzzle out the remainder of it. Impossible as it seemed, his bag was carried by some living thing. All that remained for him was to capture the thing, and recover his bag. The weak light still turned on, he gave chase.

Lad's spirits arose with a bound. His ruse had succeeded. He had reawakened in this easily-discouraged chum a new interest in the game. And he gambolled across the lawn, fairly wriggling with delight. He did not wish to make his friend lose interest again. So instead of dashing off at full speed, he frisked daintily, just out of reach of the clawing hand.

And in this pleasant fashion the two playfellows covered a hundred yards of ground. More than once, the man came within an inch of his quarry. But always, by the most imperceptible spurt of speed, Laddie arranged to keep himself and his dear satchel from capture.

Then, in no time at all, the game ended; and with it ended Lad's baby faith in the friendliness and trustworthiness of all human nature.

Realising that the sound of his own stumbling running feet and the intermittent flashes of his torch might well awaken some light sleeper in the house, the thief resolved on a daring move. This creature in front of him—dog or bear or goat, or whatever it was—was uncatchable. But by sending a bullet through it, he could bring the animal to a sudden and permanent stop.

Then, snatching up his bag and running at top speed, he himself could easily win clear of the Place before any one of the household should appear. And his car would be a mile away before the neighbourhood could be aroused. Fury at the weird beast and the wrenching strain on his own nerves lent eagerness to his acceptance of the idea.

He reached back again for his pistol, whipped it out, and, coming to a standstill, aimed at the pup. Lad, waiting only to bound over an obstruction in his path, came to a corresponding pause, not ten feet ahead of his playmate.

It was an easy shot. Yet the bullet went several inches above the obligingly waiting dog's back. Nine men out of ten, shooting by moonlight or by flashlight, aim too high. The thief had heard this old marksman-maxim fifty times. But, like most hearers of maxims, he had forgotten it at the one time in his speckled career when it might have been of any use to him.

He had fired. He had missed. In another second, every sleeper in the house and in the gate lodge would be out of bed. His night's work was a blank, unless—

With a bull rush he hurled himself forward at the interestedly waiting Lad. And, as he sprang, he fired again. Then several things happened.

Every one, except movie actors and newly-appointed policemen, knows that a man on foot cannot shoot straight, unless he is standing stock still. Yet, as luck would have it, this second shot found a mark where the first and better aimed bullet had gone wild.

Lad had leaped the narrow and deep ditch left along the lawn-edge by workers who were putting in a new water main for the Place. On the far side of this obstacle he had stopped, and had waited for his friend to follow. But the friend had not followed. Instead, he had been somehow responsible for a spurt of red flame and for a most thrilling racket.

A Dalmatian mother and her two pups resting on a doggy bed. Photo © Alan and Sandy Carey

Lad was more impressed than ever by the man's wondrous possibilities as a midnight entertainer. He waited, gaily expectant, for more. He got it.

There was a second rackety explosion and a second puff of lightning from the man's outflung hand. But, this time, something like a red-hot whip-lash smote Lad with horribly agonising force athwart the right hip.

The man had done this—the man whom Laddie had thought so friendly and playful!

He had not done it by accident. For his hand had been outflung

The cavernous yawn of a Great Dane. Photo © Alan and Sandy Carey

*"I petted [Old Yeller] and made over him till he was wiggling all over to show how happy he was.
I felt mean about how I'd treated him and did everything I could to let him know. I searched his feet
and pulled out a long mesquite thorn that had become embedded between his toes. I held him down and
had Mama hand me a stick with a coal of fire on it, so I could burn off three big bloated ticks that I
found inside one of his ears. I washed him with lye soap and water, then rubbed salty bacon grease into
his hair all over to rout the fleas. And that night after dark, when he sneaked into bed with me and
Little Arliss, I let him sleep there and never said a word about it to Mama."*
—Fred Gipson, Old Yeller, *1956*

directly at the pup, just as once had been the arm of the kennelman, back at Lad's birthplace, in beating a disobedient mongrel. It was the only beating Lad had ever seen. And it had stuck, shudderingly, in his uncannily sensitive memory. Yet now, he himself had just had a like experience.

In an instant, the pup's trustful friendliness was gone. The man had come on the Place, at dead of night, and had struck him. That must be paid for! Never would the pup forget his agonising lesson that night intruders are not to be trusted or even to be tolerated. Within a single second, he had graduated from a little friend of all the world, into a vigilant watchdog.

With a snarl, he dropped the bag and whizzed forward at his assailant. Needle-sharp milkteeth bared, head low, ruff abristle, friendly soft eyes as ferocious as a wolf's, he charged.

There had been scarce a breathing-space between the second report of the pistol and the collie's counter-attack. But there had been time enough for the onward-plunging thief to step into the narrow lip of the water-pipe ditch. The momentum of his own rush hurled the upper part of his body forward. But his left leg, caught between the ditch-sides, did not keep pace with the rest of him. There was a hideous snapping sound, a screech of mortal anguish; and the man crashed to earth, in a dead faint of pain and shock—his broken left leg still thrust at an impossible angle in the ditch.

Lad checked himself midway in his own fierce charge. Teeth bare, throat agrowl, he hesitated. It had seemed to him right and natural to assail the man who had struck him so painfully. But now this same man was lying still and helpless under him. And the sporting instincts of a hundred generations of thoroughbreds cried out to him not to mangle the defenceless.

Wherefore, he stood, irresolute; alert for sign of movement on the part of his foe. But there was no such sign. And the light bullet-graze on his hip was hurting like the very mischief.

Moreover, every window in the house beyond was blossoming forth into lights. There were sounds—reassuring human sounds. And doors were opening. His deities were coming forth.

All at once, Laddie stopped being a vengeful beast of prey; and remembered that he was a very small and very much hurt and very lonely and worried puppy. He craved the Mistress's dear touch on his wound, and a word of crooning comfort from her soft voice. This yearning was mingled with a doubt less perhaps he had been transgressing the Place's Law, in some new way; and lest he might have let himself in for a scolding. The Law was still so queer and so illogical!

Lad started toward the house. Then, pausing, he picked up the bag which had been so exhilarating a plaything for him this past few minutes and which he had forgotten in his pain.

It was Lad's collie way to pick up offerings (ranging from slippers to very dead fish) and to carry them to the Mistress. Sometimes he was

petted for this. Sometimes the offering was lifted gingerly between aloof fingers and tossed back into the lake. But, nobody could well refuse so jingly and pretty a gift as this satchel.

The Master, sketchily attired, came running down the lawn, flashlight in hand. Past him, unnoticed, as he sped toward the ditch, a collie pup limped—a very unhappy and comfort-seeking puppy who carried in his mouth a blood-spattered brown bag.

Along with a Scottish Highland bull friend, a bullmastiff poses for pictures. Photo © Kent and Donna Dannen

⧼⧽ ⧼⧽ ⧼⧽

"It doesn't make sense to me!" complained the Master, next day, as he told the story for the dozenth time, to a new group of callers. "I heard the shots and I went out to investigate. There he was lying half in and half out of the ditch. The fellow was unconscious. He didn't get his senses back till after the police came. Then he told some babbling yarn about a creature that had stolen his bag of loot and that had lured him to the ditch. He was all unnerved and upset, and almost out of his head with pain. So the police had little enough trouble in 'sweating' him. He told everything he knew. And there's a wholesale round-up of the motor-robbery bunch going on this afternoon as a result of it. But what I can't understand—"

"It's as clear as day," insisted the Mistress, stroking a silken head that pressed lovingly against her knee. "As clear as day. I was standing in the doorway here when Laddie came pattering up to me and laid a little satchel at my feet. I opened it, and—well, it had everything of value in it that had been in the safe over there. That and the thief's story make it perfectly plain. Laddie caught the man as he was climbing out of that window. He got the bag away from him; and the man chased him, firing as he went. And he stumbled into the ditch and—"

"Nonsense!" laughed the Master. "I'll grant all you say about Lad's being the most marvellous puppy on earth. And I'll even believe all the miracles of his cleverness. But when it comes to taking a bag of jewelry from a burglar and then enticing him to a ditch and then coming back here to you with the bag—"

"Then how do you account—?"

"I don't. None of it makes sense to me. As I just said. But—whatever happened, it's turned Laddie into a real watchdog. Did you notice how he went for the police when they started down the drive, last night? We've got a watchdog at last."

"We've got more than a watchdog," amended the Mistress. "An ordinary watchdog would just scare away thieves or bite them. Lad captured the thief and then brought the stolen jewelry back to us. No other dog could have done that."

Lad, enraptured by the note of praise in the Mistress's soft voice, looked adoringly up into the face that smiled so proudly down at him. Then, catching the sound of a step on the drive, he dashed out to bark in murderous fashion at a wholly harmless delivery boy whom he had seen every day for weeks.

A watchdog can't afford to relax vigilance, for a single instant—especially at the responsible age of five months.

A Rhodesian ridgeback and its owner laze away on a summer afternoon. Photo © Kent and Donna Dannen

"Happiness is dog-shaped, I say."
—*Dido, assisted by Chapman Pincher,*
My Life as a Real Dog, *1995*

Dog Training

by E. B. White

The late E. B. White was a versatile writer, to say the least. He started out as a news reporter and later took jobs in advertising, but beginning in the mid-twenties, he found his voice writing primarily humorous pieces for the upstart *New Yorker,* and is considered, along with his friend James Thurber, one of the principal reasons for the success of that publication. His first published book, however, was a book of poetry, *The Lady Is Cold*, and he would later publish more poetry; books of essays, including writing on farming, politics, the right of privacy, and the international tension gripping the world as World War II erupted across the Atlantic; and three children's books, including the classics *Stuart Little* and *Charlotte's Web*. He also revised a little book by the late William Strunk, Jr., an out-of-print volume entitled *The Elements of Style,* a title now familiar to any student of English or journalism. In 1978, he won a special Pulitzer Prize for his lifetime of writing.

"Dog Training" appeared in White's 1942 book *One Man's Meat,* written during a five-year hiatus White spent in Maine away from the New York rat race. White's essay playfully elaborates on the frustrations and joys of sharing your life with dogs.

A bulldog takes control of its daily walk and plants itself in the grass. Photo © J. Faircloth/ Transparencies, Inc.

THERE IS A book out called *Dog Training Made Easy* and it was sent to me the other day by the publisher, who rightly guessed that it would catch my eye. I like to read books on dog training. Being the owner of dachshunds, to me a book on dog discipline becomes a volume of inspired humor. Every sentence is a riot. Some day, if I ever get a chance, I shall write a book, or warning, on the character and temperament of the dachshund and why he can't be trained and shouldn't be. I would rather train a striped zebra to balance an Indian club than induce a dachshund to heed my slightest command. For a number of years past I have been agreeably encumbered by a very large and dissolute dachshund named Fred. Of all the dogs whom I have served I've never known one who understood so much of what I say or held it in such deep contempt. When I address Fred I never have to raise either my voice or my hopes. He even disobeys me when I instruct him in something that he wants to do. And when I answer his peremptory scratch at the door and hold the door open for him to walk through, he stops in the middle and lights a cigarette, just to hold me up.

"Shopping for a puppy presents a number of problems," writes Mr. Wm. Cary Duncan, author of *Dog Training Made Easy*. Well, shopping for a puppy has never presented many problems for me, as most of the puppies and dogs that have entered my life (and there have been scores of them) were not the result of a shopping trip but of an act of God. The first puppy I owned, when I was about nine years old, was not shopped for—it was born to the collie bitch of the postman of my older sister, who sent it to me by express from Washington, D. C., in a little crate containing, in addition to the puppy, a bar of Peters' chocolate and a ripe frankfurter. And the puppy I own now was not shopped for but was won in a raffle. Between these two extremes there have been many puppies, mostly unshopped for. It is not so much that I acquire dogs as it is that dogs acquire me. Maybe they even shop for me, I don't know. If they do I assume they have many problems, because they certainly always arrive with plenty, which they then turn over to me.

The possession of a dog today is a different thing from the possession of a dog at the turn of the century, when one's dog was fed on mashed potato and brown gravy and lived in a doghouse with an arched portal. Today a dog is fed on scraped beef and Vitamin B_1, and lives in bed with you.

An awful lot of nonsense has been written about dogs by persons who don't know them very well, and the attempt to elevate the purebred to a position of national elegance has been, in the main, a success. Dogs used to mate with other dogs rather casually in my day, and the results were discouraging to the American Kennel Club but entirely satisfactory to small boys who liked puppies. In my suburban town, "respectable" people didn't keep she-dogs. One's washerwoman might keep a bitch, or one's lawn cutter, but not one's next-door neighbor.

"A man down in Texas heard Pat on the radio mention the fact that our two daughters would like to have a dog. And, believe it or not, the day before we left on this campaign trip we got a message from Union Station in Baltimore saying they had a package for us. We went down to get it. You know what it was? It was a little cocker spaniel in a crate that he sent all the way from Texas. . . . And our little girl Tricia, the six year old, named it Checkers. And you know, the kids love the dog, and I just want to say this right now, that regardless of what they say about it, we're gonna keep it." —*Vice Presidential candidate Richard Nixon, commenting after being accused of accepting improper gifts, 1952.* Photo courtesy UPI/Corbis–Bettman

Above: *The Pekingese has a regal heritage; it was once forbidden for anyone but members of the Chinese royal family to own a Pekingese. This Peke, however, is just plain nutty.* Photo © Alan and Sandy Carey
Facing page: *In need of a larger umbrella, two kids and their mucky sheepdog attempt unsuccessfully to keep dry on a rainy day in the American Southwest.* Photo © Dick Dietrich

The prejudice against females made a deep impression on me, and I grew up thinking that there was something indecent and unclean about she-things in general. The word bitch of course was never used in polite families. One day a little mutt followed me home from school, and after much talk I persuaded my parents to let me keep it—at least until the owner fumed up or advertised for it. It dwelt among us only one night. Next morning my father took me aside and in a low voice said: "My son, I don't know whether you realize it, but that dog is a female. It'll have to go."

"But why does it have to?" I asked.

"They're a nuisance," he replied, embarrassed. "We'd have all the other dogs in the neighborhood around here all the time."

That sounded like an idyllic arrangement to me, but I could tell from my father's voice that the stray dog was doomed. We turned her out and she went off toward the more liberal section of town. This sort of incident must have been happening to thousands of American youngsters in those days, and we grew up to find that it had been permanently added to the record by Dorothy Parker in her short story "Mr. Durant."

On our block, in the days of my innocence, there were in addition to my collie, a pug dog, a dachshund named Bruno, a fox terrier named

German shepherds are brilliant dogs often employed as Seeing Eye dogs, military canines, and official deputies with numerous police organizations. Photo © Tara Darling

Sunny who spent many years studying one croquet ball, a red setter, and a St. Bernard who carried his mistress's handbag, shuffling along in stately fashion with the drool running out both sides of his jaws. I was scared of this St. Bernard because of his size, and never passed his house without dread. The dachshund was old, surly, and disagreeable, and was endlessly burying bones in the flower border of the DeVries's yard. I should very much doubt if any of those animals ever had its temperature taken rectally, ever was fed raw meat or tomato juice, ever was given distemper inoculations, or ever saw the whites of a veterinary's eyes. They were brought up on chicken bones and gravy and left-over cereal, and were all fine dogs. Most of them never saw the inside of their owners' houses—they knew their place.

The "problem" of caring for a dog has been unnecessarily complicated. Take the matter of housebreaking. In the suburbia of those lovely post-Victorian days of which I write the question of housebreaking a puppy was met with the simple bold courage characteristic of our forefathers. You simply kept the house away from the puppy. This was not only the simplest way, it was the only practical way, just as it is today. Our parents were in possession of a vital secret—a secret which has been all but lost to the world: the knowledge that a puppy will live and thrive without ever crossing the threshold of a dwelling house, at least till he's big enough so he doesn't wet the rug.

Although our fathers and mothers very sensibly never permitted a puppy to come into the house, they made up for this indignity by always calling the puppy "Sir." In those days a dog didn't expect anything very elaborate in the way of food or medical care, but he did expect to be addressed civilly.

Mr. Duncan discusses housebreaking at some length and assumes, as do all writers of dog books, that the owner of a puppy has little else to do except own the puppy. It is Mr. Duncan's theory that puppies have a sense of modesty and don't like to be stared at when they are doing something. When you are walking the dog, he says, you must "appear utterly uninterested" as you approach some favorite spot. This, as any city dweller knows, is a big order. Anybody who has ever tried to synchronize a puppy's bowels with a rigid office schedule knows that one's interest in the small phenomena of early morning sometimes reaches fever pitch. A dog owner may feign disinterest, but his mask will not suffice. Nothing is more comical than the look on the face of a person at the upper end of a dog leash, pretending not to know what is going on at the lower.

A really companionable and indispensable dog is an accident of nature. You can't get it by breeding for it, and you can't buy it with money. It just happens along. Out of the vast sea of assorted dogs that I have had dealings with, by far the noblest, the best, and the most important was the first, the one my sister sent me in a crate. He was an old-style collie, beautifully marked, with a blunt nose and great natural gentleness and intelligence. When I got him he was what I badly needed. I think probably all these other dogs of mine have been just a groping toward that old dream. I've never dared get another collie for fear the comparison would be too uncomfortable. I can still see my first dog in all the moods and situations that memory has filed him away in, but I think of him oftenest as he used to be right after breakfast on the back porch, listlessly eating up a dish of petrified oatmeal rather than hurt my feelings. For six years he met me at the same place after school and convoyed me home—a service he thought up himself. A boy doesn't forget that sort of association. It is a monstrous trick of fate that now, settled in the country and with sheep to take care of, I am obliged to do my shepherding with the grotesque and sometimes underhanded assistance of two dachshunds and a wire-haired fox terrier.

Facing page: *A carrot-topped Brittany staunchly pointing in the field.* Photo © Bill Buckley/The Green Agency

PART II

Canine Heroes

*"Amid the cheering of the crowds, he hardly heard his master's voice,
but he saw the familiar head and shoulders, and the bright flag he was waving. He
raced toward the seven-foot fence; without apparent effort he rose in the air and
cleared the top with a good hand-breadth to spare; then dashed up to his
master that he loved, and gamboled there and licked his hand in
heart-full joy. Again the victor's crown was his, and the master,
a man of dogs, caressed the head of shining black,
with the jewel eyes of gold."*
—Ernest Thompson Seton, *Santana, The Hero Dog of France*, 1945

Above: *From the movie* One Hundred and One Dalmatians *to its nick-
name as the firehouse dog, the Dalmatian (often called the carriage dog in
England) is a well-known hero in just about every dog-lover's book.* Photo
courtesy UPI/Corbis–Bettman
Left: *A majestic English setter points chukars in the American West.* Photo ©
William H. Mullins

The Runt

by John Taintor Foote

 Most dogs never win the gilded prize, never save a child in danger; they only set a good example for how to take a long snooze. But some dogs are our heroes. Heroism is not at all necessary to love a dog, as many of the most lovable canines in the world are scared to death of thunderclaps. But a heroic dog certainly makes for a good dog story.

John Taintor Foote knew a good dog story. In the first half of the twentieth century, he made a name for himself as a writer of outdoor fiction, penning stories for many magazines and books about dogs, horses, fishing, and more. His books include *The Look of Eagles, Pocono Shot,* and *Jing.* He also wrote several plays, and, in 1936, moved to Hollywood to work on screenplays, eventually writing such scripts as *The Mask of Zorro* and *Swanee River.*

"The Runt," which was originally published in 1917 as part of *Dumb-Bell of Brookfield* and later published in the collection *Dumb-Bell and Others,* is a heroic dog story. A thrill it is when the underdog, so to speak, does indeed bring home the gilded prize.

An adorable puppy plays in the early morning. Photo © Norvia Behling

THE KING SAT on his throne and blinked at the sunlight streaming through the French window. His eyes were pools of liquid amber filled with a brooding dignity, and kind beyond expression. His throne was a big leather chair, worn and slouchy, that stood in the bay window of the Brookfield living-room. He had slept there all night, and it was time for a maid to come, open the French window, and let him out into the dew-washed rose garden.

The king was old. He had seized the throne years before. He had been put on the train one day, with nothing but his pedigree and a prayer. He had come home, six months later, champion of champions, greatest field trial setter of his time, lion-hearted defender of the honor of Brookfield.

He never saw the inside of the kennels again. He had been given humbly the freedom of the house. After due sniffings at one place and another he had taken the leather chair for his own. From then on visitors were asked to sit elsewhere, if they didn't mind, because he might want his chair, and he was Champion Brookfield Roderigo.

So now the king sat on his throne, or rather lay curled up in it, with his long, deep muzzle resting on his paws. At the end of that muzzle was a nose. A nose uncanny in its swift certainty. A nose which had allowed him to go down wind, running like fire, stiffen in the middle of one of his effortless bounds, twist himself in the air, and light rigid at a bevy a hundred feet away. He had done this again and again when only a "derby." He had done it in the National Championship until hard-riding men, galloping behind him, had yelled like boys, and Judge Beldon, mad beyond all ethics, had called across to another judge, "The dog never lived that could beat him, Tom!"

This was a flagrant breach of form. It was unpardonable for a field trial judge to indicate his choice before the official vote. That night Judge Beldon apologized to the owner of the pointer, Rip Rap Messenger, who was running with, or rather far behind, the king at the time.

But the owner of the pointer only said: "Forget it, Judge! Why, I was as crazy as any of you. Man, oh, man, ain't he some dog!"

All this was long ago. It was no longer part of the king's life, and he was not thinking of those triumphant days of his youth. He wondered how soon the maid would come and let him out. Once in the garden he might find a toad under a rosebush at which to paw tentatively. Perhaps he would dig up the piece of dog cake he had buried in the black earth near the sundial. And there was that mole the terrier had killed, it was certainly worth a sniff or two. No doubt a gardener had removed it by this time, though . . . meddlesome things, gardeners— an unguarded bone was scarcely safe a moment when one of them was about!

Where was that maid? Why didn't she come? Perhaps he had better take a little nap. He closed his eyes. . . . He never opened them again. The heart that had pumped so stanch a beat for Brookfield decided to

Mostly hairless, a Chinese crested interprets Rachmaninoff. Photo © Tara Darling

*"For me a house or an apartment becomes a home
when you add one set of four legs, a happy tail, and that indescribable measure of love
we call a dog."*—*Roger Caras in the introduction to* Roger Caras' Treasury
of Great Dog Stories, *1987*

pump no more. A shudder passed over the king's body . . . then it was still.

The maid came presently and called his name. When he didn't stir she went to the leather chair and looked, her eyes growing wide. She hurried from the room and up the stairs.

"Mister Gregory, sir," she panted at a door, "won't you come down, please? Roderigo—he don't move. He don't move at all, sir!"

She was beside the chair again when the master of Brookfield arrived in his dressing gown.

"He don't move—" she repeated.

The master of Brookfield put his hand on the king's head. He slid his other hand under the king's body between the fore legs and held it there for a moment. Then he stooped, gathered a dangling paw, and rubbed the raspy pad of it against his cheek.

"No. He won't move—any more," he said. "Ask Mrs. Gregory to come down."

When the mistress of Brookfield came, she kneeled before the king in a patch of the streaming sunlight at which he had blinked early that morning. She kneeled a long time, twisting one of the king's soft ears between her fingers.

"He liked to have me do that," she said, looking up.

The master of Brookfield nodded.

The mistress of Brookfield bent until her lips were close to the ear she had been stroking.

"Old lover . . . old lover!" she whispered. Then she got up suddenly and went out into the rose garden.

And so there was a chair which no one ever sat in standing in the bay window of the living-room. And it was understood that the chair would remain empty until a dog was born at Brookfield who could lie in it without shame.

❧ ❧ ❧

Highland Lassie was in disgrace. Her field trial record was forgotten. She had brought three puppies into the world and had smothered two of them before they were six hours old.

"An' to think," wailed Peter, head kennel man at Brookfield, "the fussy's went en' roiled on the only Roderigo puppies this world'll ever see again! Look what she's got left—one pup, an' 'im the runt!"

He poked the pinky-white atom with a stumpy forefinger, and Highland Lassie cuddled the puppy hastily to her side.

Leona, the big blond waitress, removed a straw from Peter's coat and allowed her hand to linger on his sleeve.

"Are you not to your breakfast coming?" she asked.

But Peter had forgotten for the time that her eyes were blue, that her bosom was deep, and that she looked like gold and milk and roses.

"Breakfast?" he snorted. "An' what do I care about breakfast? 'Aven't I just told you she's gone an' killed two Roderigo *pups*, an' 'im layin' out there in the orchard?"

Facing page: *Bloodhounds are known around the world for their incredible scenting talents; they are capable of picking up a scent trail over two weeks old and following it for huge distances.* Photo © Tara Darling

"But if this be I,
As I do hope it be,
I have a little dog at home
And he knows me;
If it be I,
He'll wag his little tail,
And if it be not I
He'll loudly bark and wail!"
—Thomas Hodgkins,
"Little woman and her dog,"
1806

Leona gave a gentle tug at his sleeve.

"Always more puppies there will be," she said, and her words were like the notes of a flute.

Peter straightened up and glared at her.

"Always more puppies there will be!" he repeated with dreadful scorn. "You go back to the 'ouse!"

Leona departed with a quivering lip, to have her statement swiftly verified. That very day Black-Eyed Susan became the mother of seven, of whom Dan Gath, winner of the Manitoba All Age, was the indifferent father.

"A fine litter by a good young sire!" said Peter. "Brookfield ain't done yet. 'Ow's that for a grand pup—the second one there? 'E'll be a movin' picture, you 'ear me!"

"Maybe he'll be champion," suggested a kennel boy, hopefully.

"Champion!" said Peter. "So'll your grandmother. 'Ere, put some fresh straw in that corner an' don't you bother the bitch whilst you're doin' it, neither."

But when the boy had gone Peter filled his pipe and stared thoughtfully at Black-Eyed Susan, her eyes still fever bright from birth pangs.

"'E might at that, old gel," said Peter softly. "'E might, at that."

Four months later the second puppy in the row of seven had grown into a thing of beauty that made you gasp when you saw him. From his proudly chiseled head to the glistening plume of his tail he was a triumph.

"The grandest pup we've ever bred at Brookfield!" said Peter. "For looks, that is," he added, glancing out toward the orchard. "Only for looks."

Highland Lassie's puppy grew

Boxers are brave, clownish, fabulous with kids—and gorgeous! Photo © Alan and Sandy Carey

also. He lived in a land of plenty unshared by crowding brothers and sisters. He did not dine in frantic haste, but deliberately and at his ease, his soft-eyed mother watching.

He was seldom disturbed by callers. Even the abundance he received failed to give him size. He could add nothing, therefore, to the honor of Brookfield. He could only dim, a little, the glory of his sire— and so they let him alone.

Then weaning time came, and his mother neglected him more and more. At last she gave him up altogether, and he was left to his own devices.

He tried hard to make the time pass. A sparrow lighting in his runway was a great event. He would creep toward it, and at the proper distance would halt and stand rigid until the sparrow flew away. Some- times the sparrow would fly to a wire above the kennel and make a shadow on the ground. When this happened he pointed the shadow very carefully until it, too, was gone. Always he wished to pounce upon the sparrow, or its shadow; but he was a son of Roderigo—the great Roderigo who never flushed a bird—and so he held his point, with no one there to see.

Sparrows were few, however. They seldom came to his yard. In the long hours between their visits he was lonesome. He grew to have a wistful expression, and a grin that went to the heart. He seemed to be grinning at himself. The last son of Roderigo was a runt! It was a joke, a grim joke, and he grinned at it.

When winter withdrew at last and spring marched over the hills to Brookfield, a great washing descended upon the kennels and no one escaped.

Highland Lassie's puppy was smitten with the rest. He was taken by a kennel boy to the washroom and there he suffered in silence. The bath brought out his markings clearly, and after a casual glance at him Peter bent over and examined his left side.

"Now ain't that a curious mark?" he said. "It might 'ave been painted on 'im, it's that perfect. It's like one of them things the strong man 'olds up in the circus—I forget what you call 'em. 'E's the runt, by the old dog out of the Lassie bitch, ain't 'e?"

"Yep," said the kennel boy. "He's all alone in No. 9 runway."

"You 'aven't growed much, 'ave you?" said Peter.

The wee son of Roderigo, his eyes still smarting from carbolic soap, looked up at Peter and grinned.

Peter drew in his breath sharply.

"Bli' me!" he said. "The beggar knows. . . . Not much doin' down there in No. 9, is there? 'Ow'd you like to see the world for a while?" Once more the puppy grinned up at him.

"All right," said Peter. "I'll come an' get you when I'm through."

An hour later Peter opened the gate of runway No. 9.

"Come on out, Runt!" he said cheerfully. And the runt, for that, it seemed, was to be his name, came out. He stood for a moment, dazed

This wary Australian shepherd belies the breed's true easy-going nature. Photo © Marilyn "Angel" Wynn

by sudden freedom, then sped like an arrow far across the lawn. Peter's eyes lighted.

"'E can move!" he said. Then his face fell. "But what'll that get him?" he muttered. "'E couldn't step over a lead pencil!"

Each morning from then on the runt was let out to follow Peter about the place. Peter was in a cheerful mood these days. The master and mistress of Brookfield would soon return from Florida, and he was anticipating a triumph.

"Won't the missus squeal when she sees 'im!" he thought, as he brushed the shining coat of the Dan Gath puppy. "Eh, Runt?" he said aloud. And the runt, who had been gravely watching, grinned.

"I wish you'd quit that!" Peter told him. "It gives me the creeps!"

When at last the great day came, Peter scorned delay. The mistress of Brookfield was still in her hat and gloves when she heard that he was waiting in the rose garden.

"What does he want?" she asked. "I've hardly caught my breath!"

She was told that he had something to show her.

"Oh!" she said, and went to the terrace that looked down into the garden.

Then Peter had his triumph. He was standing at the foot of the terrace in the sunshine, and by his side was a living marvel, new washed and glistening.

Above: *An adorable pair of Yorkshire terrier puppies peer through a front-porch railing.* Photo © Alan and Sandy Carey
Facing page: *The Newfoundland is a giant among dogs, but its mellow nature belies its enormous size.* Photo © Tara Darling

The intelligent, endearing Saint Bernard is known the world round as a rescue dog. The hearty giant is named after the Saint Bernard Hospice in the Swiss Alps, where it was put to work rescuing climbers as far back as the 1600s. Photo © Alan and Sandy Carey

"To his dog, every man is Napoleon, hence the constant popularity of dogs."
—Aldous Huxley

The mistress of Brookfield stared, breathless for a moment.

"Oh, Peter!" she gasped. "He's a wonder dog! Bring him inside!"

"Yes, mem," said Peter, beaming.

"Bring him to the living-room, Peter. Mr. Gregory's in there!"

She turned to the door, failing to see that other who had followed Peter uncertainly into the rose garden. She was excited to begin with, and *he* was very small. Also, he felt that he did not belong in the sunshine beside the wonder dog; so he had hidden himself behind a rosebush and watched her through the leaves.

When they went into the house and left him, he crept up the steps, crossed the terrace, and halted at the open door. . . . Peter had gone in here with the pretty lady, and it was his habit to follow Peter. He put a timid forepaw across the threshold—nothing happened. He tried the other paw—still nothing happened. He caught the scent of Peter now, so slowly and with caution he took up the trail.

Presently he came to a big room, and saw Peter and the pretty lady and a tall man looking at the wonder dog. He wished to keep out of sight until Peter was ready to go. The recess of the bay window seemed an excellent retreat and he slipped into it. A doggy smell came to him as he did so. He advanced and found a huge chair with bulging arms and a well-hollowed seat.

He loved the chair at sight. It seemed so friendly and safe. It seemed to hold out its arms to him in welcome. Why, it actually seemed glad to see him! Perhaps it didn't know that he was a runt. . . . He curled down into its soft hollow with a deep sigh of contentment.

The master of Brookfield was still staring at the wonder dog.

"How did you do it, Peter?" he said at last. "He's too good to be true!"

"'E'll be true," said Peter, "if breedin'll do it. 'E's by Dan Gath, out of Black-Eyed Susan. You get one like 'im out of a thousand matin's—maybe."

"He's handsome enough," said the master of Brookfield. "But—what will he do in the field?"

"Listen," said Peter; "I've 'ad 'im on larks a time or two, an' I'm tellin' you now, we never bred a faster, wider, 'igher-'eaded goin' pup . . . but one." He glanced toward the leather chair, and a look of bewilderment came into his face, which changed to one of horror. "'Eavens above!" he said. "Look there!"

They followed his gaze, conscious for the first time of a strange sound which rose and fell steadily in the bay window.

Curled deep in Roderigo's chair was the runt,

There is no doubt that the dog is man's best friend. Photo © Daniel J. Cox/Natural Exposures, Inc.

and, as Peter told the kennel men afterward, "'E was snorin' that 'eavy you could 'ear 'im all through the room."

"And what the devil is that?" said the master of Brookfield, after a stunned silence.

"The runt of the last litter by the old dog," said Peter. "'E just come along."

"Yes—I see he did," said the master of Brookfield. "Come here, you!" he called.

The runt opened one eye, twitched his tail sleepily, and closed the eye again. That was all.

A whip sung in the bay window. The terrier who lived at the house could have told the runt what that whip was for. In a moment the tall man stood above him.

"Get down out of that!" he said, and flicked the whip over the chair.

The runt was frightened. The big chair was his only friend, it seemed. He shrank deeper into it as the whip was raised above him.

"Don't! Please, Jim!" said the mistress of Brookfield. "He's so little. He'll learn soon enough." She came and took the runt by his scrub. "Get down, little mannie," she said, "this place isn't for you."

"I 'ope not!" said Peter.

"Never mind, Peter," she said. "It isn't his fault that he's little, and that was his daddy's chair. . . . Oh, Jim! See that dumb-bell on his side! Look! It's perfect!"

"That's too bad!" said the master of Brookfield, examining the mark.

"Why too bad?" asked Mrs. Gregory.

The master of Brookfield winked at Peter.

"We'll never be able to lose him," he explained. "Will we?" he said to the runt, and the runt looked up and grinned.

Mrs. Gregory gave a quick little gasp.

"I hate such jokes!" she said. "Is he registered, Peter?"

"No, mem," said Peter.

"Well, register him as Brookfield Dumb-Bell—and give him every chance." Suddenly she stepped close to the runt. "You two may have the *beauty* there," she flashed; "and his missy will look after *him!*"

"Why, Chief!" said the master of Brookfield.

"I don't care!" she said. "He's little—and I think he knows it—and it isn't his fault!" Then she went out of the room.

The master of Brookfield rubbed his chin thoughtfully.

"Now what did we do, Peter?" he asked.

It was a hot summer that year. Day after day the sun glared down at Brookfield, and the runt panted as he followed Peter. Often when visitors arrived and Peter was told to bring the wonder dog to the house the runt came along.

He was always embarrassed during these visits. He felt smaller than ever in the stately rooms of the big house. But he remembered his

Facing page: *Elizabeth Taylor and Frank Morgan starring opposite Lassie in the 1946 film* The Courage of Lassie. *Photo from MGM (Courtesy Kobal)*

friend the chair, and while the visitors were exclaiming over the wonder dog he would slip away quietly and crawl into it.

He was whipped for this several times, but he never seemed to learn; so at last he was put back in runway No. 9, where there were no chairs at all, only loneliness and an occasional sparrow.

One day the master of Brookfield visited the kennels.

"Peter," he said, "ship the Dan Gath puppy to Ramsey, in Tennessee. Ship him tomorrow night. Wire Ramsey. . . . Hot, isn't it?"

"What about *'im?*" said Peter, jerking his thumb toward a runway.

"What do you mean?" asked the master of Brookfield. Then he saw the occupant of No. 9 staring wistfully out at Peter.

"Oh!" he said, "*you* break him this fall for a shooting dog. He ought to have a nose on him."

As Peter was going over a dog crate next day, he looked up to find the mistress of Brookfield watching him.

"Good morning, Peter," she said. "What's that crate for?"

"I'm shippin' the Dan Gath pup away tonight, mem," said Peter. "'E's to 'ave a chance at the trials."

"Why have you brought out only one crate?" asked the mistress of Brookfield.

"I'm only shippin' one dog," said Peter, tapping away with his hammer.

"Ah!" said she. "And when does the runt go?"

"'E don't go," said Peter. "I'm to break 'im myself—for a shootin' dog."

"Peter!" said the mistress of Brookfield.

"Yes, mem," said Peter uneasily.

"Get out another crate, please." And when two crates stood side by side, the mistress of Brookfield touched one of them with her finger tips.

"The little chap," she said, "goes in this crate tonight. Do you understand me, Peter?"

"Yes, mem," said Peter.

"And, Peter—tell Ramsey to send the training bills to me."

"Yes, mem," said Peter.

Two weeks later the mails brought a letter to Brookfield. It was addressed to Peter, and this is how it ran:

Emeryville, Tennessee, R. R. No. 4
Sept. 6, 19—

Friend Peter:
I take shame in telling you the small pup is lost. He found a bevy the first day I took him out, chased when they flushed, and I ain't seen him since. I've hunted the country over and offered big rewards. Tell Mrs. Gregory, and say a good word for me. The big pup is doing fine. I like every move he makes.

I'll keep on looking for the little pup, and that's all at present.
Yours in friendship,
W. Ramsey.

Peter sat on a sawhorse and slowly read his letter. He moved to an overturned grindstone, seeking a better light, and read it again. He looked up toward the house, a black pile against the setting sun, and whistled softly.

"'Ell will be to pay shortly," he muttered, and moved reluctantly to his doom.

The master of Brookfield had been to the cattle barns to watch the milking. When he returned he found that Peter was something of a prophet. He found his lady bathed in tears, Peter standing miserably before her, and maids running in all directions.

"I'm going to Tennessee tonight!" she gasped. "Read that!"

"But, Chief!" said the master of Brookfield when he had read the letter. "You couldn't possibly do any good down there. If Ramsey, who knows every foot of the country, can't find him, how can you expect to?"

"I'll send down a motor and ride all day," she told him. "You can come too—and Peter—and Felix to drive . . ."

Golden retrievers are a favorite to serve as Seeing Eye dogs, therapy dogs, and assisted-living aides.
Photo © Keith Baum

A Brussels griffon (known outside of the United States as the griffon Bruxellois) bats an adorable brown eye on a warm summer day. Photo © Alan and Sandy Carey

"Is that all?" he said. "We'll be quite a party. It's out of the question, my dear. . . . I'll tell Ramsey to double the reward and do everything possible. . . . You'll make yourself sick if you don't stop crying!"

"We *have* lost him, you see! Inspite of your horrid joke about it. *Now* I hope you and Peter are satisfied! I'll write to Ramsey!" she added ominously. "Oh, I'll write to *him!*"

When W. Ramsey, Esq., received a letter a few days later he whistled over it much as Peter had whistled over his.

"I guess I'd better quit trainin'," he muttered, "an' go to pup huntin' for a perfession!"

And until he went West with his "string," the redoubtable Bill Ramsey, high-priced specialist in the training and handling of field trial

setters, turned his field work and yardbreaking over to an assistant, and scoured the country day after day. But no one had seen a "real small setter with a funny mark on his side," and he never found a trace of what he sought.

※ ※ ※

Brookfield Beau Brummell No. 43721 F. D. S. B., for such was now the wonder dog's official title, was taken to a country where he could go far, and fast, and wide.

In the cramped valleys and thicket-rimmed fields of the East, bobwhite lives close to cover, and field trial dogs are educated in the land of the prairie chicken, where their handlers can keep them in sight for mile after level mile.

The Beau was put down one morning with the veteran Rappahannock as guide, counselor, and friend. The sun was beginning to climb the eastern side of the huge blue void which domed an ocean of grass.

"Hi, yah! Get away!" yelled Ramsey. Rappahannock, free of the leash, shot over a gentle rise and was gone. He had eaten up a good half-mile of country when the frostbitten grass began to whisper just behind him. He flattened out in a desperate effort to shake off the whisper, but the whisper grew to the soft pad, pad of toying feet, as the Beau, moving like oil, flowed past.

Ramsey lowered his field glasses and smiled.

"Look out for that one, Mike!" he called to his assistant. "They've bred another bird dog at Brookfield!"

As time went on and the Beau developed into a prodigy of speed, range, and nose, Peter went about his work with a far-away look in his eyes. His body was at Brookfield, his spirit in Manitoba. The Beau would make his first start in the great Canadian stake, and—"They can't beat him!" was the word that came from Ramsey.

On the day the stake was run Peter sat on the grindstone and

> *"Scratch a dog and you'll find a permanent job."*
> *—Franklin P. Jones*

whittled. He spoke no word to anyone. Late in the evening the telephone bell rang in the kennels, but Peter never stirred. A kennel boy
approached him timidly.

"They want you up to the house," said the boy; and Peter closed
his knife and rose.

He found the mistress of Brookfield in the living-room. Her
cheeks were flushed, her eyes like stars. She was dancing about the
master of Brookfield with a fluttering telegram in her hand.

"Peter!" she said, *"Oh, Peter! See what our boy's done!"*

Peter read the telegram, then looked at the master of Brookfield
through half shut lids.

"If they don't watch 'im 'e'll likely take the National," he said.

"It's possible," said the master of Brookfield. "Yes, it's possible."

"Why, of course," said Mrs. Gregory. "Didn't you know that? He's
to be champion. . . . Outclassed his field!" she sang. "Did you read that,
Peter? Read it again."

This was only the beginning. The Beau swept through field trial
after field trial, piling victory upon victory. He won again in Canada.
He came nearer home, into Illinois, to take the Independent All Age
from the best dogs in the land. He went down into Georgia, and left
his field gasping behind him in the select Continental. He won "off by
himself," as Ramsey said, in the Eastern Subscription against twenty-
five starters, and "every dog worth a million dollars!"

He was certain to take the National. No other dog could stand his
pace in the three-hour running of the Championship. Rival handlers
conceded this, and Black-Eyed Susan came into her own.

"Susan is trying not to look down on the rest of us, Peter," explained the mistress of Brookfield.

Peter watched Black-Eyed Susan partake of crackers and cream
languidly, and from a silver spoon.

"I can't say as 'ow you're 'elpin' 'er much," he said.

Then suddenly Ramsey was smitten with inflammatory rheuma-
tism, and the Beau was turned over to Scott Benson, who would
handle him in his other engagements.

"Don't worry," Peter told the master of Brookfield. "Scott's a good
'andler. It's all over, anyway, but the United States *and* the Championship. . . . Are you goin' down?"

"To the National? Why, yes," said the master of Brookfield. He
caught a wistful look in Peter's eyes. "Would *you* care to go?" he asked.

Peter bent over and picked up a willow twig for whittling pur-
poses.

"Why, I expect the boys could look after things here for a day or
two," he said.

The United States All Age was the last big stake before the Championship. On the morning after it was run, Peter was whistling as he
sprinkled the whelping shed with disinfectant. Footsteps crunched on
the gravel outside and he stepped to the door. The master of Brookfield

A pawprint in the sand along an Alaskan seashore. Photo © Lon E. Lauber

"Of any beast, none is more faithful found
Nor yeelds more pastime in house, plaine, or woods,
Nor keepes his master's person, nor his goods,
With greater care, than doth the dog or hound."
—*Joachim Camerarius,* Living Librarie, *1583*

stood there with a newspaper in his hand.

"He was beaten, Peter," he said.

"*No!*" said Peter. And after a silence—"What beat 'im?"

"Little Sam," said the master of Brookfield.

"An' who is Little Sam?" asked Peter.

"I don't know," said the master of Brookfield. "I never heard of him before. Our dog was second. Here! Read it yourself."

The dispatch was short:

Grand Junction, Tenn., Jan. 8.

In the All Age stake of the United States Field Trial Club, Little Sam, lemon and white setter, handled by C. E. Todd, was first. Brookfield Beau Brummell, black, white, and ticked setter, handled by Scott Benson, was second. Thirty-two starters.

"C. E. Todd!" said Peter. "Why, that's Old Man Todd—'e's eighty years old if 'e's a day! What's 'e doin' back in the game?"

"Don't ask me!" said the master of Brookfield. "He's back, it would seem, and he's brought a dog."

"Do you think 'e'll start 'im in the National?" Peter inquired.

"I presume so," said the master of Brookfield. "You're to bring the Beau home, Peter—if he wins."

"An' if 'e don't—win?" asked Peter.

"Why, then," said the master of Brookfield, "he can stay in training and try again next year."

Three days later the mistress of Brookfield stood with Black-Eyed Susan in the high stone arch of the front entrance. "You're to bring home the champion, Peter!" she called. "Don't fail us, will you?—Susy and me? There's some light underwear in the black bag, Jim; it may be warm in Tennessee. Good-by. . . . Good-by, Peter. . . . Your shaving things are in the small bag, Jim! Peter—Peter! Don't forget Susy and me—we'll be waiting!"

"No, mem," said Peter stoutly. But as he watched the landscape slide steadily northward the ties clicked a fearsome refrain: *"Little Sam!"* they said, *"Little Sam!"*

Grand Junction was reached at last. Scott Benson was the first to greet them at the packed and roaring hotel.

"Well," said the master of Brookfield, "how does it look?"

The trainer shook his head.

"Bad, Mr. Gregory," he said. "We've got an awful dog to beat."

"You mean the dog that old Todd's got?" said Peter.

"Yes," said Scott. "That's what I mean—but he ain't a dog."

"What is 'e, then?" asked Peter.

"He's a flying machine, with a telescope nose. You got a grand dog, Mr. Gregory, a grand dog. A gamer dog never lived—he'll try all the way; but this here dog that old fool's got a hold of somehow ain't

This young girl is perhaps a little more enthusiastic than her golden about exchanging affections. Photo © Norvia Behling

human. In three hours he'll find all the quail in the state!"

"What's 'e look like, an' 'ow's 'e bred?" Peter inquired.

"Get ready to laugh," said Scott. "I forgot to tell you. His breedin's unknown, an' he ain't as big as a stud beagle."

That evening was a trial. Beau Brummell seemed forgotten. The hotel lobby echoed with the name of Little Sam.

"He must be a great dog," smiled the master of Brookfield. "I'll enjoy seeing him run. I think I'll turn in now, Major, if you'll excuse me. I'm a little tired from the trip."

Peter sat up longer, half listening to the babble about him. At last he became conscious of a hissing for silence as the secretary climbed to a table top and began to read the drawings for the National.

"Belwin with Dan's Lady!" read the secretary. "Opal Jane with Rappahannock! Bingo with Prince Rodney!" and so the starters in the Championship were paired. At last, at the very end, the secretary paused an instant and smiled grimly. "Brookfield Beau Brummell with Little Sam!" he read, and there was a roar that shook the hotel.

Chuck Sellers leaped upon Peter and took him to his bosom.

"Stick around, Pete!" he yelled. "Stick around fur the big show!"

Peter shoved him aside.

"I'm goin' to bed," he growled. "I 'ope I get a decent 'oss tomorrow."

But fate had a blow in store for Peter. In the scramble for mounts

A tiny bichon frisé and a dachshund puppy share a corner of a child's chair.
Photo © Alan and Sandy Carey

next morning, a big gray mule with a will of his own was "wished on him" as Chuck Sellers put it, and he devoted the next few hours to equestrianship. By the time the second brace was cast off he had conquered, and he saw good old Rappahannock win on his courage from dashing Opal Jane, who failed to last the three hot hours and was running slower and slower, with a dull nose, when they took her up.

The Championship was run off smoothly. Brace after brace was put down, until at last came Thursday morning and the pair for which they waited.

Peter had been having an argument with his mount, who hated to start in for the day. When it was settled he looked up to see an old man standing ahead of the judges, with a lemon and white setter who tugged and tugged to be gone. He was small beyond belief, this setter, so small that Peter rubbed his eyes. Then he rode down the line of horsemen until he found Chuck Sellers.

"Don't tell me that's 'im, Chuck?" he said.

"That's him," said Chuck.

"Why, a bunch of grass'll stop 'im!" said Peter. "'E ain't big enough to jump it."

"*He* don't jump nothin'," Chuck informed him. "He's got wings."

"'E may lose 'em before three hours," said Peter. "'Im an' 'is breedin' unknown."

"Maybe," said Chuck. "Here's the dog to clip 'em, or it can't be done," and he pointed to Beau Brummell going out to his position.

He was still the wonder dog, a glory every inch of him, and a murmur of admiration rippled down the line of horsemen. . . . Peter felt a sudden glow of pride and hope.

But it didn't last. The next moment he was watching a white speck fade away across the stubble. As it grew dimmer and dimmer so did Peter's hopes. The white speck was Little Sam, breeding unknown. When he whirled and came to point, at the far edge of the woods, Brookfield Beau Brummell was a hundred feet behind.

Peter was among the stragglers in the stampede across the field which followed. When he reached the mass of waiting horsemen, Old Man Todd was being helped out of his saddle to shoot over his dog.

With a feeling of numb despair Peter looked for the master of Brookfield. He saw him at last, sitting his horse a little apart from the crowd, his face the color of ashes.

Peter rode to him quickly.

"What's the matter, sir?" he asked. "Are you unwell?"

The master of Brookfield kept his eyes on the pointing dog.

"*Look!*" he said, "*look!*" And Peter looked at Little Sam. Then his heart skipped a beat, fluttered, and sent the blood surging against his eardrums.

Little Sam had his bevy nailed. He stood as though of stone. He looked like white marble against the dark of the woods. And on his side, his left and nearest side, was a perfect lemon dumb-bell. . . .

An American Staffordshire terrier is ready for a day of fishing. Photo © Kent and Donna Dannen

"My Gawd," said Peter. "My Gawd."

He swung his eyes along the woods and found another statue. It was Beau Brummell, still as death itself, in honor of his brace mate.

"My Gawd!" said Peter again. "What'll we do?"

"Nothing—*now*," said the master of Brookfield. "Let the best dog win."

A man should only whisper while the championship is run, but Peter rose in his stirrups, not fifty feet from a brace on point, and disgraced himself forever.

"My money's on the old dog's blood," he howled; *"an' let the best dog win!"*

"Peter! Peter!" said the master of Brookfield, and took him by the arm.

"I forgot," said Peter sheepishly.

There have been field trials in the past, there will be field trials in the future. But those who saw the whirlwind struggle between the great Beau Brummell and the white ghost with the magic nose will not listen while you tell of them. Eighteen bevies they found that day, and they went at top speed to do it. Not a bird was flushed as they flashed into point after dazzling point, backing each other like gentlemen.

"The best thing about man is the dog."
—*Pierre-Laurent Buyrette de Belloy,* Le Siège de Calais, *1765*

It was perfect bird work, done with marvelous speed, and the Beau had the sympathy of those who watched, for they knew that he was beaten. He had everything that makes a champion, including looks and heart. But the little white dog who skimmed from one covey to the next was more than a champion—he was a miracle. The blazing soul of Roderigo had leaped to life in this, his son, and would not be denied.

An hour or more had passed when Chuck Sellers thought of Peter and sought him out to offer what consolation he could.

"The little dog may quit, Pete," he said, "any time now. It's the last half that tells on the short-bred ones."

Then Peter gave the puzzled Chuck a wide calm smile.

"Nothing is certain in this 'ere world," he said. "But I'll tell you one thing that is. That little dog won't quit till the pads wear off his feet."

And Peter was right. The announcement of the new champion finished with "breeding unknown."

The crowd swarmed toward the winner, who grinned as they closed about him. They had never seen a National Champion without a pedigree, and they pushed and pulled and laughed and hooted.

A *Field* reporter was yelling at Old Man Todd above the noise.

"The country wants to know this dog's breeding, old man," he said. "And it's got to be traced, if possible."

"He ain' got no breedin', I tell you!" screamed Old Man Todd. "He's a niggah-raised dawg—jes' a niggah-raised dawg!"

The runt was frightened. It must be terrible to be a nigger-raised dog, or all these men wouldn't glare at him and yell! He remembered leaving the place where the big house was, long ago, and riding on a train. He remembered running for miles and miles until he had found that nice shed where he could rest. A black man had come to the shed and given him some milk. He drank it all and went to sleep.

Next he remembered hunting birds with the black man every day. One day an old man had watched him find some birds and had talked with the black man. Then he was taken away by the old man, and had hunted birds with him ever since.

They had had a good hunt today. But now he was tired, and they all yelled at him so. Then someone pushed and fought his way through the crowd, and the runt was glad to see him, for it was Peter, whom he had followed long ago.

The runt went to him quickly, and Peter fell on one knee and put an arm about him.

"Runt!" said Peter. "Runt!—You're yer daddy's own son!"

The runt grinned, and Peter put him down and took hold of the leash.

"Let go of this, Old Man," he said.

It is not a good thing to win the championship with a "niggah-raised" dog when that dog has been advertised over an entire state as lost. Old Man Todd looked into Peter's eyes.

"Why—why—" he began, and stopped. Then his fingers unclosed from the leash and he backed slowly into the crowd.

Peter whirled about and faced the reporter, with the runt close at his side.

"Now, Mr. Reporter," he said, "you can put in your paper that Brookfield Dumb-Bell by Champion Brookfield Roderigo 'as won the National. You can say the new champion is out of Brookfield 'Ighland Lassie. You can tell 'em 'e was bred and whelped at Brookfield—and now 'e's goin' 'ome."

The reporter was dancing up and down. His face was red and he had lost his hat.

"How can I verify this?" he yelled. "How can I verify this?"

Suddenly the runt saw the tall man who lived in the big house he dimly remembered. He had always been afraid of the tall man—he was so quiet. He was quiet now. He didn't yell at all, but when he held up his hand everybody kept still.

"I can verify it for you," he said.

"Mr. Gregory!" said the reporter. "Good, very good—excellent! Will you let me have the facts as quickly as possible, please? I've got to catch the evening papers!"

Peter didn't stay to hear what the tall man said, and the runt was glad for he was tired. But Peter put him on a train and he couldn't sleep it jiggled so, and the baggage man gave him part of his supper. When other men came into the car, the baggage man pointed to him and said something about "National Champion," and "worth ten thousand dollars," and the men came and stared at the runt.

At last they got out of the train, and he and Peter and the tall man rode in an automobile till they went through some gates, and the runt saw the lights of the big house shining through the trees.

A terrier checks out what's going on from the edge of a cast-iron bed.
Photo © Alan and Sandy Carey

"Where shall I take him," asked Peter, "to the kennels?"

The tall man dropped his hand on the runt's head.

"I think not, Peter," he said; and they all got out at the front door.

As they came into the hall someone called from upstairs, and the runt recognized the voice of the pretty lady.

"Oh, Jim!" said the voice. "Why didn't you wire? Did Beau Brummell win?"

"No," said the tall man. "He was runner up."

"Oh!" said the voice, and then nothing more for a while, and the runt could hear the big clock ticking in the hall.

"Is Peter there?" said the voice at last.

"Yes, mem," said Peter.

"You went back on Susy and me, didn't you, Peter?" said the voice.

"Come down here, Chief!" said the tall man. "Unleash him!" he directed in a low voice, and Peter did so.

The runt threw up his head and sniffed. He was so tired by now that his legs were beginning to shake, and he wanted a place to lie down . . . then suddenly he remembered. He walked to the living-room and peered in. . . . Yes, there was his friend the chair, holding out its arms to him. . . . The runt gave a deep sigh as he curled himself into it.

The tall man who had followed laughed softly.

"And *that's* all right!" he said.

Just then the pretty lady came in.

"Why—what dog is that?" she asked.

"Don't you know?" said the tall man.

The pretty lady stared at the runt very hard. He became uneasy, and grinned. The pretty lady shrieked and ran to him.

"Little mannie!" she said, hugging him until he could feel her heart beating against his side. "Where did they find you, little mannie?"

"At Grand Junction," said the tall man.

"What was he doing there?" asked the pretty lady.

"A good deal," said the tall man.

The pretty lady gave the runt a last big squeeze, then she straightened up.

"Oh, Runt!" she said. "Darling Runt—you're just as bad as ever!" She put her hand on his collar. "Come!" she said. "This place isn't for you."

But the tall man stepped forward, and took her hand from the collar. His eyes were shining queerly and his voice was husky.

"Let him alone, my dear!" he said. "Let him alone!"

It was nice of the tall man to do this, thought the runt. He must have known how tired, how very tired, he was. He curled himself deep in the chair and began to snore. . . . In his dreams he heard the tall man talking, and then the pretty lady bent above him, and a wet drop fell on his nose.

Facing page: *Yuri, a Siberian husky, rests up after a long day pulling a sled.* Photo © Jack Macfarlane

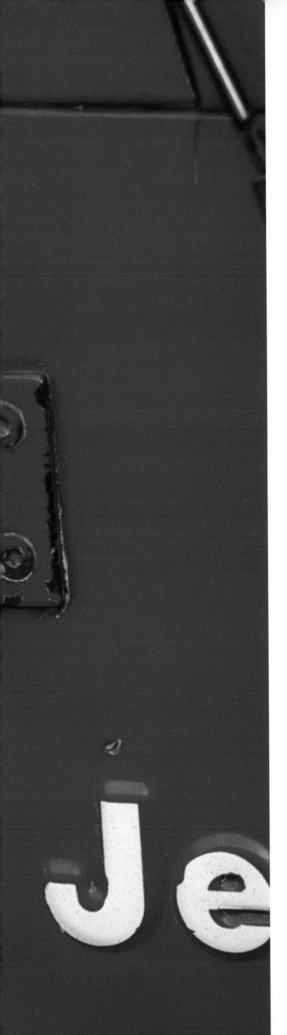

PART III

Best Friend

"I know that I have had friends who would never have vexed or betrayed me, if they had walked on all fours."
— The 4th Earl of Orford, Horace Walpole, British Historian and Writer

Above: *A Boston terrier gets a ride in the sporty wheels of its diminutive owner.* Photo © J.C. Allen & Son, Inc., West Lafayette, Indiana, USA
Left: *Through thick and thin, a dog will remain by your side—or even under your feet like this West Highland white terrier.* Photo © Kent and Donna Dannen

Intelligent and Loyal

by Jilly Cooper

 Loyalty is often hard to come by; just about every individual has their own motivations, values, ways of treating people. But individuals with fur and a wagging tail operate by a different set of guidelines. Czechoslovakian writer Karel Čapek in his book *I Had a Dog and a Cat* put it most succinctly, writing: "I affirm, to their masters men preserve a servile and gloomy relation, while a dog with his master possesses a relationship of passionate, reckless love." That unconditional love—and the dog's immediate and permanent acceptance of you as "master of the domain"—goes a long way toward explaining why dogs are nearly universally considered our best friends.

Jilly Cooper has published dozens of books over a career that spans more than forty years. A diverse writer, her published work includes several collections of newspaper columns, titles about relationship issues such as *Work and Wedlock*, a book about the British class system, titles such as *On Rugby* and *On Cricket*, several novels, and numerous works of juvenile fiction.

"Intelligent and Loyal" is an excerpt from her book *Intelligent and Loyal: A Celebration of the Mongrel*. Cooper's mutts all have a deep connection to their masters, in some instances the attachment is so remarkable it seems to prove the existence of a sixth sense.

"Deep down in [the dog's] consciousness as the spiritual sign of distinction was the fact that he belonged to a superior race—the only race in the animal kingdom which preferred the society of man to that of its own kind."—Arthur Sherburne Hardy, Peter, 1920. Photo © Henry H. Holdsworth/Wild by Nature

MANY MONGRELS HAVE a remarkable ability to distinguish different days of the week and others are excellent timekeepers. A dog is a creature of routine with a built-in time clock. Perhaps the same kind of instinct tells birds it is time to migrate when the days start getting shorter.

What is less easy to explain is how so many dogs anticipate the arrival of their master or mistress even when they don't turn up at a regular time. One mongrel owner, who jets around the world a great deal, said that at first her dog missed her dreadfully when she left home but after a day or two settled into a routine with the housekeeper, of whom he was very fond. Whenever his mistress returned home, however, the moment her plane landed the dog sensed it, and started screaming with excitement. He wouldn't settle until her car finally drew up at the front door.

Kim Spink, a sleek Standard Magpie with a badger stripe down his forehead, always knew when any of the family would be coming home. They all turned up at different times of the day, and there was no routine about this, but Kim always stationed himself at the stairs window, ten minutes before each arrival.

Kim had the badger stripe which seems to be a characteristic of dogs with second sight. He also had a Borderline Collie mother, and mongrels with Collie blood also seem to be particularly psychic. Susie Bill, a red Fetcher, and Ben her stable mate, a smooth black Satin Crammer, always took up their positions on a chair by the window a quarter of an hour before their master returned home—whatever time he arrived. As he worked eight miles away, it was as though they sensed the exact time he left work. When Mr Bill's mother died, he went over to her house to sort out her things, telling his wife he'd be home by seven. During the afternoon he rang to say, there was so much to do he wouldn't be back until long after nine. At six forty-five, the dogs took up their lookout positions on their chair.

'You'll have a long wait,' warned Mrs Bill, but sure enough at seven o'clock Mr Bill arrived, having decided to abandon sorting for the day and come home after all.

The sceptic would insist that the dogs recognize the sound of their owner's car, and also have far superior hearing to humans, but surely this hearing would not be acute enough to pick up a car leaving a quarter of an hour's drive away. Nor does this explain the behaviour of a Rough Diamond called Judy Brown, who lives in a shop where cars are pulling up all day, but who only barks at her master's car, although she can't see him arriving from inside the shop. Nor is it the sound of the engine she recognizes, as she barked the first time he turned up in a new car. She also barks before the telephone rings.

Another inexplicable phenomenon is the mongrel's ability to select the right bus. Bully Latchford, a stalwart rugby player, like many a man before him got bored when he was taken shopping by his mistress and used to sneak off and take the 93 bus home. He always went upstairs and was a great favourite with the conductors. He knew it was time to

Childhood just wouldn't be right without a family hound by your side. Photo © Norvia Behling

"How true it is that dogs reflect the character of their masters!
A noisy, blustering windbag of a man inevitably has a dog that rushes out to roar at
everything that will give ground to him. The dour chap possesses a sullen beast of kind, and your hail-
fellow sort of person usually owns a merry member of the tail-waggers that considers all
passers-by friends."—Paul A. Curtis, Sportsmen All, *1938*

get off when the bus levelled out at the top of the hill, but, and this is the remarkable part, although there were two bus routes from the town shops, Bully always caught the right bus.

Miss Ellen Coath also remembers a Bertrand Russell called Bobby who was a great wanderer. He used to take free rides from the village, to the end of the road, where Miss Coath lived. One day when she was already on the bus, she saw him board it, run upstairs, crawl under a front seat, then jump out at the right stop. There were two buses which took different routes from Beckenham, but Bobby, like Bully, always took the right one.

Even more impressive at the turn of the century were the navigational skills of a mongrel called Kruger Rogerson.

"He was owned by my dad's Uncle Jim," writes Mr Rogerson, "who was a road paver and always took Kruger to work. Each morning Uncle Jim caught a Stockport tram from Cheadle Heath to Mersey Square in the centre of Stockport, changed trams to take another six mile ride to Hyde Town Hall, then caught a train to Mottram. On several occasions Kruger overslept after a night on the tiles, but nothing daunted would set off, catch all the necessary connections, and get to work only half an hour after his master. All the conductors knew him. On his collar was stamped, 'I am Kruger Rogerson, who the hell are you?'"

When Mrs Margaret Turner was a child before the war, she had a little Terrier called Raggy who always picked her up on time from school, and whose bump of locality was as good as his time clock. Every Saturday night he took a train to the other side of Huddersfield to visit an old lady who gave him chocolate biscuits, then caught the right train home again. It must have been easier for dogs in those days when there was less traffic, and no one kicked up a queenie fuss if a stray dog joined them in a bus or train carriage. Raggy's bump of locality also stood him in good stead during a family outing, when he got lost on the moors seven miles from home. Margaret sobbed and sobbed, thinking she'd never see her dog again, but when the family got back home there was Raggy wagging on the doorstep. He was probably guided home by scent, but there are extraordinary tales of dogs finding their way home after travelling to a strange place by car.

Bobby, a two-and-a-half-year-old mongrel belonging to a French florist in the town of La Ferte Alais, got lost in the flower market in the heart of Paris. After a fruitless search his master returned sadly home. Yet five days later an exhausted Bobby arrived on the doorstep. He had covered thirty-five miles and, even more impressive, this rural dog had found his way out of Paris, one of the busiest and most geographically complicated cities in the world.

Dogs who travel to a place by car must notice landmarks on the way. During the war Mr Sharpe, who lived in Finchley, used to drive the family and their dog Chum along a labyrinth of back roads to visit his in-laws in Wood Green. One day Chum, a sleek Standard Magpie

Facing page: Irish setters were bred as gun dogs, and the red setter is quite capable in the field. But Irish setters pretty much love everybody, which means they also find a very warm reception in any family. Photo © Tara Darling

with the inevitable badger streak down his forehead, vanished after a bitch. The family searched everywhere, but like the French florist had to return home to Finchley empty-handed. At two-thirty in the morning they were overjoyed to hear a faint scratch on the back door. Bedraggled, exhausted and desperately thirsty, Chum had come the fifteen miles home.

Sometimes by returning to base by a circuitous route a stray mongrel wins its spurs and is allowed to stay. Mr Hutchings tells a touching story of the Standard Magpie bitch he and his sister found wandering in the market when they were children.

"We were convinced it was Floss, our neighbour's bitch. She wagged her tail so hard when we called her that we found an old piece of rope and took her home by tram. When we reached our neighbour's house she was amazed, because her own Floss was already in residence. We realized the two pups were identical. Mother insisted we took our Floss back, so tearfully we boarded the tram and took her back to market. We kept looking back hoping she might follow us, but she didn't. To our delight, when we got home we found her waiting. Mother relented, and she became a member of our family for ten years."

Whatever good fairy guided Floss and the other dogs back home was aided by the fact that the dogs had been to the place at least once before. Some dogs may have a homing instinct, like carrier pigeons, and are able to navigate by the angle of the sun or the stars. If a dog is separated from home (or the place he considers he ought to be) his internal clock tells him there is an incongruity between the time of day he feels inside him, and the time of day the sun is registering by virtue of its position. He then sets out in the direction that will reduce this internal and external difference. Once he gets near home, he will pick up familiar smells and sights and find his way home easily.

What is far more difficult to explain is how dogs trace owners to places where the dog has never been. There was for example a mongrel in the First World War who, never having been out of England before, crossed the channel and found his master in the trenches. Then there was the mongrel called Tony, who was left in the care of friends because his owners had moved from Illinois to a town in Michigan some 225 miles away. Somehow, six weeks later, Tony, wearing his identifying collar and disc, turned up at the Michigan home. Such feats must defy the rational mind and it is here we enter the tricky world of ESP or "Psi-trailing," as it is called, which means the psychic location of where someone is. Perhaps in the same way that the mongrel in Australia "knew" his mistress had landed, Tony and the dog in the First World War were drawn by some sixth sense to their owners. T.S. Eliot wrote of lovers "who think the same thoughts without need of speech." Perhaps dogs, whose devotion exceeds that of most lovers, are able to pick up telepathic vibrations from beloved owners who are constantly thinking and worrying about them.

Brave, intelligent Doberman pinschers are fabulous guard dogs. Photo © Alan and Sandy Carey

*"Humans have externalized their wisdom—
stored it in museums, libraries, the expertise of the learned. Dog wisdom is
inside the blood and bones."—Donald McCaig,*
Nop's Trials, *1984*

Hermann

by James Herriot

 Veterinarian James Alfred Wight enjoyed his privacy, undoubtedly one of the reasons, in addition to a great love of animals, that he decided to pursue a career as a country veterinarian. It is also the reason he adopted the pseudonym James Herriot—a moniker adopted after the name of a particularly talented soccer player he happened to see while working on a story and watching a match on television. Under the new pen name, Herriot published his first book, *If Only They Could Talk*, in 1970 at age fifty. The book sold modestly in the United Kingdom.

Two years later, he published his second book, also sold only in the United Kingdom, *It Shouldn't Happen to a Vet*. But St. Martin's Press released both of Herriot's books in a single volume in the United States that same year, under the title *All Creatures Great and Small*, and the modest, pseudonymous Herriot quickly became one of the best-known and most-beloved veterinarians in the world; a film version of *All Creatures Great and Small* in 1974, starring Anthony Hopkins and Simon Ward, certainly helped in this vein. Herriot went on to write *Let Sleeping Vets Lie* and *Vet in Harness* (released as a single volume in the United States as *All Things Bright and Beautiful*), *Vets Might Fly* and *Vet in a Spin* (released together in America under the title *All Things Wise and Wonderful*), *The Lord God Made Them All*, and several more books, including a travel essay about his Yorkshire homeland and several children's titles.

"Hermann," from *The Lord God Made Them All*, is a wonderful story, filled with love and humility in vintage Herriot style.

A Pomeranian puppy keeps close to its owner's heart. Photo © Marilyn "Angel" Wynn

"WAS THERE NO peace in a vet's life?" I wondered fretfully as I hurried my car along the road to Gilthorpe village. Eight o'clock on a Sunday evening and here I was, trailing off to visit a dog ten miles away which, according to Helen who had taken the message, had been ailing for more than a week.

I had worked all morning then spent an afternoon in the hills with the children and some of their friends, a long-standing weekly event during which we had managed to explore nearly every corner of the district over the years. Jimmy had set a brisk pace with his hardy young pals and I had had to carry Rosie on my shoulders up the steepest slopes. After tea there was the usual routine of baths, story reading and bed for the two of them, then I was ready to settle down with the Sunday papers and listen to the radio.

Yet here I was back on the treadmill, staring through the windscreen at the roads and the walls that I saw day in, day out. When I left Darrowby, the streets of the little town were empty in the gathering dusk and the houses had that tight-shut, comfortable look that raised images of armchairs and pipes and firesides, and now, as I saw the lights of the farms winking on the fell-sides, I could picture the stocksmen dozing contentedly with their feet up.

I had not passed a single car on the darkening road. There was nobody out but Herriot.

I was really sloshing around in my trough of self-pity when I drew up outside a row of greystone cottages at the far end of Gilthorpe. Mrs. Cundall, Number Four, Chestnut Row, Helen had written on the slip of paper, and as I opened the gate and stepped through the tiny strip of garden, my mind was busy with half-formed ideas of what I was going to say.

"Humans are aware of very little, it seems to me, the artificial brainy side of life, the worries and bills and the mechanisms of jobs, the doltish psychologies we've placed over our lives like a stencil. A dog keeps his life simple and unadorned. He is who he is, and his only task is to assert this."—Brad Watson, Last Days of the Dog-Men, *1996*
Photo © Lon E. Lauber

A hand-colored photo of the A.O. Olson kids of Milton, North Dakota, spending an afternoon in the park with their hard-working mutt, circa 1907. Photo courtesy Fred Hultstrand History in Pictures Collection, NDIRS-NDSU, Fargo

"When a dog wags his tail and barks at the same time,
how do you know which end to believe?"—Anonymous

My few years' experience in practice had taught me that it did no good at all to remonstrate with people for calling me out at unreasonable times. I knew perfectly well that my words never seemed to get through to them and that they would continue to do exactly as they had done before, but for all that I had to say something, if only to make me feel better.

No need to be rude or ill-mannered, just a firm statement of the position: that vets liked to relax on Sunday evenings just like other people; that we did not mind at all coming out for emergencies, but that we did object to having to visit animals that had been ill for a week.

I had my speech fairly well prepared when a little middle-aged woman opened the door.

"Good evening, Mrs. Cundall," I said, slightly tight-lipped.

"Oh, it's Mr. Herriot." She smiled shyly. "We've never met, but I've seen you walkin' round Darrowby on market days. Come inside."

The door opened straight into the little low-beamed living room, and my first glance took in the shabby furniture and some pictures framed in tarnished gilt when I noticed that the end of the room was partly curtained off.

Mrs. Cundall pulled the curtain aside. In a narrow bed a man was lying, a skeleton-thin man whose eyes looked up at me from hollows in a yellowed face.

"This is my husband, Ron," she said cheerfully, and the man smiled and raised a bony arm from the quilt in greeting.

"And here is your patient, Hermann," she went on, pointing to a little dachshund who sat by the side of the bed.

"Hermann?"

"Yes, we thought it was a good name for a German sausage dog." They both laughed.

"Of course," I said. "Excellent name. He looks like a Hermann."

The little animal gazed up at me, bright-eyed and welcoming. I bent down and stroked his head, and the pink tongue flickered over my fingers.

I ran my hand over the glossy skin. "He looks very healthy. What's the trouble?"

"Oh, he's fine in himself," Mrs. Cundall replied. "Eats well and everything, but over the last week he's been goin' funny on 'is legs. We weren't all that worried but tonight he sort of flopped down and couldn't get up again."

"I see. I noticed he didn't seem keen to rise when I patted his head." I put my hand under the little dog's body and gently lifted him onto his feet. "Come on, lad," I said. "Come on, Hermann, let's see you walk."

As I encouraged him he took a few hesitant steps, but his hind end swayed progressively, and he soon dropped into the sitting position again.

"It's his back, isn't it?" Mrs. Cundall said. "He's strong enough on 'is forelegs."

"That's ma trouble, too," Ron murmured in a soft husky voice, but he was smiling, and his wife laughed and patted the arm on the quilt.

I lifted the dog onto my knee. "Yes, the weakness is certainly in the back." I began to palpate the lumbar vertebrae, feeling my way along, watching for any sign of pain.

"Has he hurt 'imself?" Mrs. Cundall asked. "Has somebody hit 'im? We don't usually let him out alone, but sometimes he sneaks through the garden gate."

"There's always the possibility of an injury," I said. "But there are other causes." There were, indeed—a host of unpleasant possibilities. I did not like the look of this little dog at all. This syndrome was one of the things I hated to encounter in canine practice.

"Can you tell me what you really think?" she said. "I'd like to know."

"Well, an injury could cause haemorrhage or concussion or oedema—that's fluid—all affecting his spinal cord. He could even have a fractured vertebra, but I don't think so."

"And how about the other causes?"

"There's quite a lot. Tumours, bony growths, abscesses or discs can press on the cord."

Above: *It is my experience that in some areas [my poodle] Charley is more intelligent than I am, but in others he is abysmally ignorant. He can't read, can't drive a car, and has no grasp of mathematics. But in his own field of endeavor, which he was now practicing, the slow, imperial smelling over and anointing of an area, he has no peer. Of course his horizons are limited, but how wide are mine?"*—John Steinbeck, from Travels with Charley in Search of America, *1962.* Photo © Norvia Behling

Facing page: *A cocker in casual attire waits patiently while its master watches a holiday parade.* Photo © Kent and Donna Dannen

A beautiful Brittany watches as the daylight recedes. Photo © Lon E. Lauber

"Discs?"

"Yes, little pads of cartilage and fibrous tissue between the vertebrae. In long-bodied dogs like Hermann, they sometimes protrude into the spinal canal. In fact, I think that is what is causing his symptoms."

Ron's husky voice came again from the bed. "And what's 'is prospects, Mr. Herriot?"

Oh, that was the question. Complete recovery or incurable paralysis. It could be anything. "Very difficult to say at this moment," I

replied. "I'll give him an injection and some tablets, and we'll see how he goes over the next few days."

I injected an analgesic and some antibiotic, and counted out some salicylate tablets into a box. We had no steroids at that time. It was the best I could do.

"Now, then, Mr. Herriot." Mrs. Cundall smiled at me eagerly. "Ron has a bottle o' beer every night about this time. Would you like to join 'im?"

"Well . . . it's very kind of you, but I don't want to intrude . . ."

"Oh, you're not doing that. We're glad to see you."

She poured two glasses of brown ale, propped her husband up with pillows and sat down by the bed.

"We're from south Yorkshire, Mr. Herriot," she said.

I nodded. I had noticed the difference from the local accent.

"Aye, we came up here after Ron's accident, eight years ago."

"What was that?"

"I were a miner," Ron said. "Roof fell in on me. I got a broken back, crushed liver and a lot o' other internal injuries, but two of me mates were killed in the same fall, so ah'm lucky to be 'ere." He sipped his beer. "I've survived, but Doctor says I'll never walk no more."

"I'm terribly sorry."

"Nay, nay," the husky voice went on. "I count me blessings, and I've got a lot to be thankful for. Ah suffer very little, and I've got t'best wife in the world."

Mrs. Cundall laughed. "Oh, listen to 'im. But I'm right glad we came to Gilthorpe. We used to spend all our holidays in the Dales. We were great walkers, and it was lovely to get away from the smoke and the chimneys. The bedroom in our old house just looked out on a lot o' brick walls, but Ron has this big window right by 'im and he can

> *"I think we are drawn to dogs because they are the uninhibited creatures we might be if we weren't certain we knew better."*
> *—George Bird Evans,*
> *"Troubles with Bird Dogs"*

see for miles."

"Yes, of course," I said. "This is a lovely situation." The village was perched on a high ridge on the fell-side, and that window would command a wide view of the green slopes running down to the river and climbing high to the wildness of the moor on the other side. This sight had beguiled me so often on my rounds, and the grassy paths climbing among the airy tops seemed to beckon to me. But they would beckon in vain to Ron Cundall.

"Gettin' Hermann was a good idea, too," he said. "Ah used to feel a bit lonely when t'missus went into Darrowby for shoppin', but the little feller's made all the difference. You're never alone when you've got a dog."

I smiled. "How right you are. What is his age now, by the way?"

"He's six," Ron replied. "Right in the prime o' life, aren't you, old lad?" He let his arm fall by the bedside, and his hand fondled the sleek ears.

"That seems to be his favourite place."

"Aye, it's a funny thing, but 'e allus sits there. T'missus is the one who has to take 'im for walks and feeds 'im, but he's very faithful to me. He has a basket over there but this is 'is place. I only have to reach down and he's there."

This was something that I had seen on many occasions with disabled people: that their pets stayed close by them as if conscious of their role of comforter and friend.

I finished my beer and got to my feet. Ron looked up at me. "Reckon I'll spin mine out a bit longer." He glanced at his half-full glass. "Ah used to shift about six pints some nights when I went out wi' the lads but you know, I enjoy this one bottle just as much. Strange how things turn out."

His wife bent over him, mock-scolding. "Yes, you've had to right your ways. You're a reformed character, aren't you?"

They both laughed as though it were a stock joke between them.

"Well, thank you for the drink, Mrs. Cundall. I'll look in to see Hermann on Tuesday." I moved towards the door.

As I left I waved to the man in the bed, and his wife put her hand on my arm. "We're very grateful to you for comin' out at this time on a Sunday night, Mr. Herriot. We felt awful about callin' you, but you understand it was only today that the little chap started going off his legs like that."

"Oh, of course, of course, please don't worry. I didn't mind in the least."

And as I drove through the darkness I knew that I didn't mind— now. My petty irritation had evaporated within two minutes of my entering that house, and I was left only with a feeling of humility. If that man back there had a lot to be thankful for, how about me? I had everything. I only wished I could dispel the foreboding I felt about his dog. There was a hint of doom about those symptoms of Hermann's,

A young owner goofs around with her equally young yellow Lab in a field of wildflowers. Photo © Layne Kennedy

*"It did not take Man long—probably not more than a
hundred centuries—to discover that all the animals except the dog were impossible
around the house. One has but to spend a few days with an aardvark or a llama, command a water
buffalo to sit up and beg, or try to housebreak a moose, to perceive how wisely Man set about
his process of elimination and selection."—James Thurber,
"An Introduction" to Thurber's Dogs, 1955*

The handsome English pointer is a top-notch gun dog. Photo © Bill Buckley/The Green Agency

and yet I knew I just had to get him right. . . .

On Tuesday he looked much the same, possibly a little worse.

"I think I'd better take him back to the surgery for X-ray," I said to Mrs. Cundall. "He doesn't seem to be improving with the treatment."

In the car Hermann curled up happily on Rosie's knee, submitting with good grace to her petting.

I had no need to anaesthetise him or sedate him when I placed

him on our newly acquired X-ray machine. Those hind quarters stayed still all by themselves—a lot too still for my liking.

I was no expert at interpreting X-ray pictures, but at least I could be sure there was no fracture of the vertebrae. Also, there was no sign of bony extoses, but I thought I could detect a narrowing of the space between a couple of the vertebrae, which would confirm my suspicions of a protrusion of a disc.

Laminectomy or fenestration had not even been heard of in those days, so I could do nothing more than continue with my treatment, and hope.

By the end of the week, hope had grown very dim. I had supplemented the salycilates with long-standing remedies like tincture of nux vomica and other ancient stimulant drugs, but when I saw Hermann on the Saturday he was unable to rise. I tweaked the toes of his hind limbs and was rewarded by a faint reflex movement, but with a sick certainty I knew that complete posterior paralysis was not far away.

A week later, I had the unhappy experience of seeing my prognosis confirmed in the most classical way. When I entered the door of the Cundalls' cottage,

Hermann came to meet me happy and welcoming in his front end but dragging his hind limbs helplessly behind him.

"Hello, Mr. Herriot." Mrs. Cundall gave me a wan smile and looked down at the little creature stretched frog-like on the carpet. "What d'you think of him now?"

I bent and tried the reflexes. Nothing. I shrugged my shoulders, unable to think of anything to say. I looked at the gaunt figure in the bed, the arm outstretched as always on the quilt.

"Good morning, Ron," I said as cheerfully as I could, but there was no reply. The face was averted, looking out of the window. I walked over to the bed. Ron's eyes were staring fixedly at the glorious panorama of moor and fell, at the pebbles of the river, white in the early sunshine, at the criss-cross of the grey walls against the green. His face was expressionless. It was as though he did not know I was there.

I went back to his wife. I don't think I have ever felt more miserable.

"Is he annoyed with me?" I whispered.

"No, no, no, it's this." She held out a newspaper. "It's upset him something awful."

I looked at the printed page. There was a large picture at the top, a picture of a dachshund exactly like Hermann. This dog, too, was paralysed, but its hind end was supported by a little four-wheeled bogie. In the picture it appeared to be sporting with its mistress. In fact, it looked quite happy and normal, except for those wheels.

Ron seemed to hear the rustle of the paper because his head came round quickly. "What d'ye think of that, Mr. Herriot? D'ye agree with it?"

"Well . . . I don't really know, Ron. I don't like the look of it, but I suppose the lady in the picture thought it was the only thing to do."

"Aye, maybe." The husky voice trembled. "But ah don't want Hermann to finish up like that." The arm dropped by the side of the bed and his fingers felt around on the carpet, but the little dog was still splayed out near the door. "It's 'opeless now, Mr. Herriot, isn't it?"

"Well, it was a black lookout from the beginning," I said. "These cases are so difficult. I'm very sorry."

"Nay, I'm not blamin' you," he said. "You've done what ye could, same as the vet for that dog in the picture did what 'e could. But it was no good, was it? What do we do now—put 'im down?"

"No, Ron, forget about that just now. Sometimes paralysis cases just recover on their own after many weeks. We must carry on. At this moment I honestly cannot say there is no hope."

I paused, then turned to Mrs. Cundall. "One of the problems is the dog's natural functions. You'll have to carry him out into the garden for that. If you gently squeeze each side of his abdomen, you'll encourage him to pass water. I'm sure you'll learn how to do that."

"Oh, of course, of course," she replied. "I'll do anything. As long as there's some hope."

Facing page: *A Pembroke Welsh corgi would gladly slip his whole body through the space between the fence slats if it could, but will have to settle for only a nose poke for at least a small taste of the world beyond the walls.* Photo © Norvia Behling

Kids and dogs were made for each other. Photo © Norvia Behling

"There is, I assure you, there is."

But on the way back to the surgery, the thought hammered in my brain. That hope was very slight. Spontaneous recovery did sometimes occur, but Hermann's condition was extreme. I repressed a groan as I thought of the nightmarish atmosphere that had begun to surround my dealings with the Cundalls. The paralysed man and the paralysed dog. And why did that picture have to appear in the paper just at this very time? Every veterinary surgeon knows the feeling that fate has loaded the scales against him, and it weighed on me, despite the bright sunshine spreading into the car.

However, I kept going back every few days. Sometimes I took a couple of bottles of brown ale along in the evening and drank them with Ron. He and his wife were always cheerful, but the little dog never showed the slightest sign of improvement. He still had to pull his useless hind limbs after him when he came to greet me, and, though he always returned to his station by his master's bed, nuzzling up into Ron's hand, I was beginning to resign myself to the certainty that one day that arm would come down from the quilt and Hermann would not be there.

It was on one of these visits that I noticed an unpleasant smell as I entered the house. There was something familiar about it.

I sniffed, and the Cundalls looked at each other guiltily. There was a silence, and then Ron spoke.

"It's some medicine ah've been givin' Hermann. Stinks like hell, but it's supposed to be good for dogs.

"Oh, yes?"

"Aye, well . . ." His fingers twitched uncomfortably on the bedclothes. "It was Bill Noakes put me onto it. He's an old mate

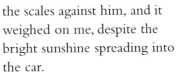

"The dog without his master was like modesty with raiment, like a body without a soul."—Mary E. Wilkins Freeman, *"The Lost Dog" from* Understudies, *1900*

o' mine—we used to work down t'pit together—and he came to visit me last weekend. Keeps a few whippets, does Bill. Knows a lot about dogs, and 'e sent me this stuff along for Hermann."

Mrs. Cundall went to the cupboard and sheepishly presented me with a plain bottle. I removed the cork, and as the horrid stench rose up to me, my memory became suddenly clear. Asafoetida, a common constitutent of quack medicines before the war and still lingering on the shelves of occasional chemist shops and in the medicine chests of people who liked to doctor their own animals.

I had never prescribed the stuff myself, but it was supposed to be beneficial in horses with colic and dogs with digestive troubles. My own feeling had always been that its popularity had been due solely to the assumption that anything which stank as badly as that must have some magical properties, but one thing I knew for sure was that it could not possibly do anything for Hermann.

I replaced the cork. "So you're giving him this, eh?"

Ron nodded. "Aye, three times a day. He doesn't like it much but Bill Noakes has great faith in it. Cured hundreds o' dogs with it, 'e says." The deep-sunk eyes looked at me with a silent appeal.

"Well, fine, Ron," I said. "You carry on. Let's hope it does the trick."

I knew the asafoetida couldn't do any harm, and since my treatment had proved useless I was in no position to turn haughty. But my main concern was that these two nice people had been given a glimmer of hope, and I wasn't going to blot it out.

Mrs. Cundall smiled and Ron's expression relaxed. "That's grand, Mr. Herriot," he said. "Ah'm glad ye don't mind. I can dose the little feller myself. It's summat for me to do."

It was about a week after the commencement of the new treatment that I called in at the Cundall's as I was passing through Gilthorpe.

"How are you today, Ron?" I asked.

"Champion, Mr. Herriot, champion." He always said that, but today there was a new eagerness in his face. He reached down and lifted his dog onto the bed. "Look 'ere."

He pinched the little paw between his fingers, and there was a faint but definite retraction of the leg. I almost fell over in my haste to grab at the other foot. The result was the same.

"My God, Ron," I gasped. "The reflexes are coming back."

He laughed his soft, husky laugh. "Bill Noakes's stuff's working, isn't it?"

A gush of emotions, mainly professional shame and wounded pride welled in me, but it was only for a moment. "Yes, Ron," I replied. "It's working. No doubt about it."

He stared up at me. "Then Hermann's going to be all right?"

"Well, it's early days yet, but that's the way it looks to me."

It was several weeks more before the little dachshund was back to

A couple of chocolate Lab pups sharpen their young molars on a stick. Photo © Alan and Sandy Carey

*"The one absolutely unselfish friend that man
can have in this selfish world, the one that never deserts him,
the one that never proves ungrateful or treacherous, is his dog."*
—*Senator Graham Vest,* Eulogy on the Dog

normal, and, of course, it was a fairly typical case of spontaneous recovery, with nothing whatever to do with the asafoetida or, indeed, with my own efforts. Even now, thirty years later, when I treat these puzzling back conditions with steroids, broad-spectrum antibiotics and sometimes colloidal calcium, I wonder how many of them would have recovered without my aid. Quite a number I imagine.

Sadly despite the modern drugs, we still have our failures, and I always regard a successful termination with profound relief.

But that feeling of relief has never been stronger than it was with Hermann, and I can recall vividly my final call at the cottage in Gilthorpe. As it happened, it was around the same time as my first visit—eight o'clock in the evening—and when Mrs. Cundall ushered me in, the little dog bounded joyously up to me before returning to his post by the bed.

"Well, that's a lovely sight," I said. "He can gallop like a racehorse now."

Ron dropped his hand down and stroked the sleek head. "Aye, isn't it grand? By heck, it's been a worryin' time."

"Well, I'll be going." I gave Hermann a farewell pat. "I just looked in on my way home to make sure all was well. I don't need to come anymore now."

"Nay, nay," Ron said. "Don't rush off. You've time to have a bottle o' beer with me before ye go."

I sat down by the bed, and Mrs. Cundall gave us our glasses before pulling up a chair for herself. It was exactly like that first night. I poured my beer and looked at the two of them. Their faces glowed with friendliness, and I marvelled because my part in Hermann's salvation had been anything but heroic.

In their eyes everything I had done must have seemed bumbling and ineffectual, and, in fact, they must be convinced that all would have been lost if Ron's old chum from the coal face had not stepped in and effortlessly put things right.

At best, they could only regard me as an amiable fathead, and all the explanations and protestations in the world would not alter that. But though my ego had been bruised, I did not really care. I was witnessing a happy ending instead of a tragedy, and that was more important than petty self-justification. I made a mental resolve never to say anything that might spoil their picture of this triumph.

I was about to take my first sip when Mrs. Cundall spoke up. "This is your last visit, Mr. Herriot, and all's ended well. I think we ought to drink some sort o' toast."

"I agree," I said. I looked around for an inspiration, and on a far shelf my eye caught a glimpse of the asafoetida bottle. The memory of its stench lanced briefly at my nose, defying me to put my humbled resolution to the test. "I have just the right toast," I said, raising my glass. "Here's to Bill Noakes."

Facing page: *"He is very imprudent, a dog is. He never makes it his business to inquire whether you are in the right or in the wrong, never bothers as to whether you are going up or down life's ladder, never asks whether you are rich or poor, silly or wise, sinner or saint. You are his pal."—Jerome K. Jerome,* Idle Thoughts for an Idle Fellow, *1889.* Photo © Bill Buckley/The Green Agency

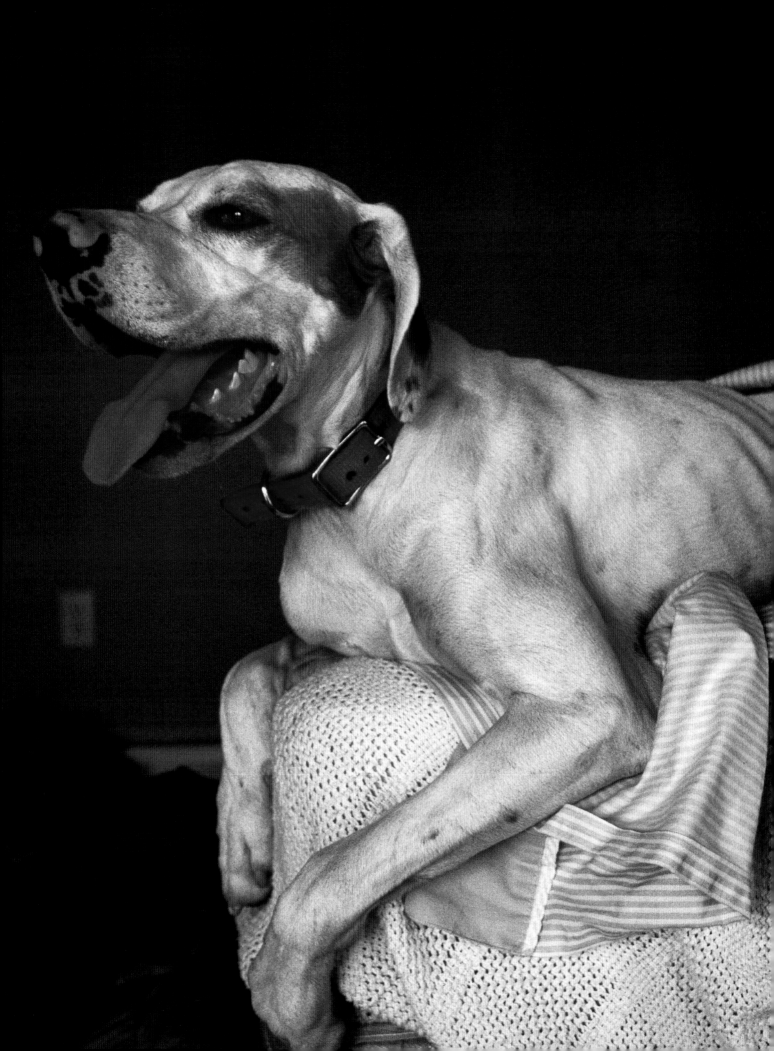

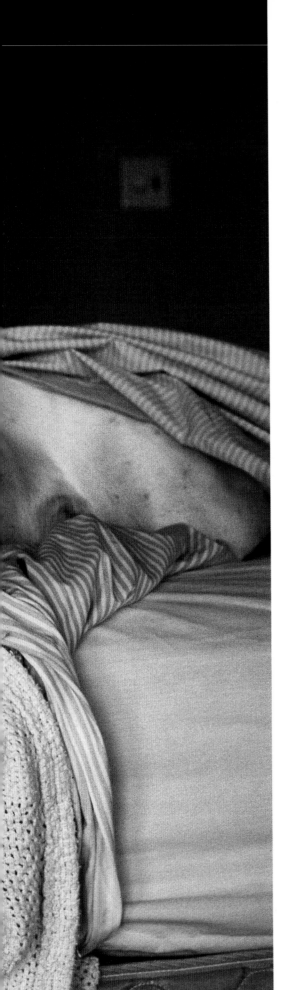

PART IV

Love Me, Love My Dog

*"My dog! the difference between thee and me
Knows only our Creator."*
—Alphonse Marie Louis de Prat de Lamartine, French Poet

Above: *The Marguerite Kirmse etching* Day Dreams. Courtesy of the AKC Museum of the Dog
Left: *Friends and family of dog owners must accept the hound of the house, a canine that sometimes enjoys access to every corner of a dog lover's home.* Photo © Bill Buckley/The Green Agency

Moses

by Walter D. Edmonds

 Your dog is a part of you. Certainly, any relationship can result in conflict if the other person cannot accept an aspect of yourself: your predilection for knock-knock jokes, your lisp, your bum knee, the fact that you love to eat pig's feet. But if they don't accept your dog, waste no time in showing your friend the door. If they own the house, take your dog and run.

Known primarily for his works of historical fiction, Walter D. Edmonds is the author of more than twenty novels and juvenile works, three histories, and some sixty short stories. His work has been published in the *Atlantic Monthly*, *Harper's*, the *Saturday Evening Post*, *Scribner's Magazine*, *McCall's*, and other publications, and perhaps his best-known book, *Drums Along the Mohawk* (1936), found its way to the Hollywood big screen in 1939.

"Moses" originally appeared in the *Atlantic Monthly* in 1938 and came out in book form that same year. It was reissued in 1954 under the title *Hound Dog Moses in the Promised Land*, with illustrations by William Gropper. The former owner of this hound certainly goes to extremes because he loves his dog, and, in the process, all of eternity adjusts to accommodate the bond.

A lovable mutt laying in a piazza in Venice. Photo © Art Wolfe

IT WAS A long climb. The scent was cold, too; so faint that when he found it behind the barn he could hardly trust himself. He had just come back from Filmer's with a piece of meat, and he had sat down behind the barn and cracked it down; and a minute later he found that scent reaching off, faint as it was, right from the end of his nose as he lay.

He had had the devil of a time working it out at first, but up here it was simple enough, except for the faintness of it. There didn't appear to be any way to stray off this path; there wasn't any brush, there wasn't any water. Only he had to make sure of it, when even for him it nearly faded out, with so many other stronger tracks overlaying it: His tail drooped, and he stumbled a couple of times, driving his nose into the dust. He looked gaunt when he reached the spot where the man had lain down to sleep.

The scent lay heavier there. He shuffled round over it, sifting the dust with an audible clapping of his nostrils to work out the pattern the man had made. It was hard to do, for the dust didn't take scent decently. It wasn't like any dust he had ever come across, either, being glittery, like mica, and slivery in his nose. But he could tell after a minute how the man had lain, on his back, with his hands under his head, and probably his hat over his eyes, to shield them from the glare which was pretty dazzling bright up this high, with no trees handy.

His tail began to cut air. He felt better, and all of a sudden he lifted up his freckled nose and let out a couple of short yowps and then a good chest-swelled belling. Then he struck out up the steep going once more. His front legs may have elbowed a little, but his hind legs were full of spring, and his tail kept swinging

That was how the old man by the town entrance saw him, way down below.

The old man had his chair in the shadow of the wall, with a black and yellow parasol tied to the back of it as an extra insurance against the sun. He was reading the Arrivals in the newspaper, the only column that ever interested him; but he looked up sharply when he heard the two yowps and the deep chest notes that, from where he sat, had a mysterious floating quality. It was a little disturbing; but when he saw a dog was the cause he reached out with his foot and shoved the gate hard, so that it swung shut and latched with a sound like a gong. Only one dog had ever come here, and that sound had been enough to discourage him; he had hung round for a while, though, just on the edge, and made the old man nervous. He said to himself that he wasn't going to watch this one, anyway, and folded the paper in halves the way the subway commuter had showed him and went on with the Arrivals.

After a while, though, he heard the dog's panting coming close and the muffled padding of his feet on the marble gate stone. He shook the paper a little, licked his thumb, and turned over half a sheet and read on through the Arrivals into the report of the Committee on Admissions. But then, because he was a curious old man, and kind-hearted, noticing

A gorgeous golden in an indigo field of wildflowers. Photo © Lynn M. Stone

*"Say something idiotic
and nobody but a dog politely wags his tail."*
—*Virginia Graham,* Everything's Too
Something!, *1966*

that the panting had stopped,—and because he had never been quite up to keeping his resolves, except once—he looked out of the gate again.

The dog was sitting on the edge of the gate stone, upright, with his front feet close under him. He was a rusty-muzzled, blue-tick fox-hound, with brown ears, and eyes outlined in black like an Egyptian's. He had his nose inside the bars and was working it at the old man.

"Go away," said the old man. "Go home."

At the sound of his voice, the hound wrinkled his nose soberly and his tail whipped a couple of times on the gate stone, raising a little star dust.

"Go home," repeated the old man, remembering the dog that had hung around before.

He rattled the paper at him, but it didn't do any good. The dog just looked solemnly pleased at the attention, and a little hopeful, and allowed himself to pant a bit.

"This one's going to be worse than the other," the old man thought, groaning to himself as he got up. He didn't know much about dogs anyway. Back in Galilee there hadn't been dogs that looked like this one—just pariahs and shepherds and the occasional Persian grey-hound of a rich man's son.

He slapped his paper along the bars; it made the dog suck in his tongue and move back obligingly. Peter unhooked his shepherd's staff from the middle crossbar, to use in case the dog tried to slip in past him, and let himself out. He could tell by the feeling of his bare ankles that there was a wind making up in the outer heavens and he wanted to get rid of the poor creature before it began really blowing round the walls. The dog backed off from him and sat down almost on the edge, still friendly, but wary of the shepherd's staff.

"Why can't the poor dumb animal read?" thought Peter, turning to look at the sign he had hung on the gatepost.

The sign read:—

TAKE NOTICE

NO

DOGS

SORCERERS

MURDERERS

IDOLATERS

LIARS

WILL BE ADMITTED

He had taken the listing out of Revelations and he had thought, when he put it up, that it might save him a lot of trouble; but it certainly wasn't going to help in the case of this dog. He expected he would have to ask the Committee on Admissions to take the matter up; and he started to feel annoyed with them for not having got this

Facing page: Miss Jane Bowles *(1775) by Joshua Reynolds.* Reproduced by permission of the Trustees of the Wallace Collection, London

animal on the list themselves. It was going to mean a lot of correspondence and probably the Committee would send a memorandum to the Central Office suggesting his retirement again, and Peter liked his place at the gate. It was quiet there, and it was pleasant for an old man to look through the bars and down the path, to reassure the frightened people, and, when there was nothing else to do, to hear the winds of outer heaven blowing by.

"Go away. Go home. Depart," he said, waving his staff; but the dog only backed down on to the path and lay on his wishbone, with his nose between his paws.

II

Peter went inside and sat down and tried to figure the business out. There were two things he could do. He could notify the Committee of the dog's arrival, or he could give the information to the editor. The Committee would sit up and take notice for once if they found the editor had got ahead of them. It would please the editor, for there were few scoops in Heaven. And then, as luck would have it, the editor himself came down to the gate.

The editor wasn't Horace Greeley or anybody like that, with a reputation in the newspaper world. He had been editor of a little country weekly that nobody in New York, or London, or Paris had ever heard of. But he was good and bursting with ideas all the time. He was now.

"Say, Saint Peter," he said, "I've just had a swell idea about the Arrivals column. Instead of printing all the 'arrivals' on one side and then the 'expected guests' on the other, why not just have one column and put the names of the successful candidates in upper-case type? See?" He shoved a wet impression under Peter's nose and rubbed the back of his head nervously with his inkstained hand. "Simple, neat, dignified."

Peter looked at the galley and saw how simple it would be for him, too. He wouldn't have to read the names in lower case at all. It would make him feel a lot better not to know. Just check the upper-case names as they came to the gate.

He looked up at the flushed face of the editor, and his white beard parted over his smile. He liked young, enthusiastic men, remembering how hard, once, they had been to find.

A motley menagerie of dogs, evidently with problems to discuss, assemble around the truck of a canine behaviorist. Photo © Kent and Donna Dannen

Sometimes, the bigger the dog, the more love it has to offer. This Great Dane is not at all shy about expressing its love for its owner. Photo © Michael Brinneman/Transparencies, Inc.

"Folk will know how large your soul is,
By the way you treat a dog!"
—Charles F. Doran

"The almighty who gave the dog to be companion of our pleasure and our toils hath invested him with a nature both noble and incapable of deceit. He forgets neither friend nor foe; he remembers with accuracy, both benefit and injury. He hath a share of man's intelligence but no share of man's falsehood. You may bribe an assassin to slay a man, or a witness to take his life, by false accusation, but you cannot make a dog tear his benefactor. He is the friend of man, save when man justly incurs his enmity."
—*Sir Walter Scott*

"It looks fine to me, Don," he said. "But the Committee won't like losing all that space in the paper, will they?"

"Probably not," the editor said ruefully. "But I thought you could pull a few wires with the Central Office for me."

Peter sighed.

"I'll try," he said. "But people don't pay attention to an old man, much, Don. Especially one who's been in service."

The editor flushed and muttered something about bums.

Peter said gently, "It doesn't bother me, Don. I'm not ashamed of the service I was in." He looked down at his sandals. He wondered whether there was any of the dust of that Roman road left on them after so long a time. Every man has his one great moment. He'd had two. He was glad he hadn't let the second one go. "I'll see what I can do, Don."

It was a still corner, by the gate; and, with both of them silently staring off up the avenue under the green trees to where the butterflies were fluttering in the shrubbery of the public gardens, the dog decided to take a chance and sneak up again.

He moved one foot at a time, the way he had learned to do behind the counter in the Hawkinsville store, when he went prospecting toward the candy shelf. These men didn't hear him any more than the checker players in the store did, and he had time to sniff over the gatepost thoroughly. It puzzled him; and as the men didn't take any notice, he gumshoed over to the other post and went over that, too.

It was queer. He couldn't smell dog on either of them and they were the best-looking posts he had ever come across. It worried him some. His tail drooped and he came back to the gate stone and the very faint scent on it, leading beyond the

A rottweiler in a Montana field. Photo © Alan and Sandy Carey

gate, that he had been following so long. He sat down again and put his nose through the bars, and after a minute he whined.

It was a small sound, but Peter heard it.

"That dog," he said.

The editor whirled round, saying, "What dog?" and saw him.

"I was going to let you know about him, only I forgot," said Peter. "He came up a while ago, and I can't get rid of him. I don't know how he got here. The Committee didn't give me any warning and there's nothing about him in the paper."

"He wasn't on the bulletin," said the editor. "Must have been a slip-up somewhere."

"I don't think so," said Peter. "Dogs don't often come here. Only one other since I've been here, as a matter of fact. What kind of a dog is he anyway? I never saw anything like him." He sounded troubled and put out, and the editor grinned, knowing he didn't mean it.

"I never was much of a dog man," he said. "But that's a likely-looking foxhound. He must have followed somebody's scent up here. Hi, boy!" he said. "What's your name? Bob? Spot? Duke?"

The hound lowered his head a little, wrinkled his nose, and wagged his tail across the stone.

"Say," said the editor, "why don't I put an ad in the Lost and Found? I've never had anything to put there before. But you better bring him in and keep him here till the owner claims him."

"I can't do that," said Peter. "It's against the Law."

"No dogs. Say, I always thought it was funny there were no dogs here. What happens to them?"

"They get removed," said Peter. "They just go."

"That don't seem right," the young editor said. He ruffled his back hair with his hand. "Say, Saint, who made this law anyway?" he asked.

"It's in Revelations. John wasn't a dog man, as you call it. Back in Galilee we didn't think much of dogs, you see. They were mostly pariahs."

"I see," said the editor. His

"... it sometimes takes days, even weeks, before a dog's nerves tire. In the case of terriers it can run into months."—E. B. White, One Man's Meat, 1939. Photo © Kent and Donna Dannen

blue eyes sparkled. "But say! Why can't I put it in the news? And write an editorial? By golly, I haven't had anything to raise a cause on since I got here."

Peter shook his head dubiously.

"It's risky," he said.

"It's a free country," exclaimed the editor. "At least nobody's told me different. Now probably there's nothing would mean so much to the owner of that dog as finding him up here. You get a genuine dog man and this business of passing the love of women is just hooey to him."

"Hooey?" Peter asked quietly.

"It just means he likes dogs better than anything. And this is a good dog, I tell you. He's cold-tracked this fellow, whoever he is, Lord knows how. Besides, he's only one dog, and look at the way the rabbits have been getting into the manna in the public garden. I'm not a dog man, as I said before, but believe me, Saint, it's a pretty thing on a frosty morning to hear a good hound high-tailing a fox across the hills."

Adorable dalmatian pups play around with a soccer ball in a summer dandelion field. Photo © Alan and Sandy Carey

"We don't have frost here, Don."

"Well," said the editor, "frost or no frost, I'm going to do it. I'll have to work quick to get it in before the forms close. See you later."

"Wait," said Peter. "What's the weather report say?"

The editor gave a short laugh.

"What do you think? Fair, moderate winds, little change in temperature. Those twerps up in the bureau don't even bother to read the barometer any more. They just play pinochle all day, and the boy runs that report off on the mimeograph machine."

"*I* think there's a wind making up in the outer heavens," Peter said. "When we get a real one, it just about blows the gate stone away. That poor animal wouldn't last a minute."

The editor whistled. "We'll have to work fast." Then, suddenly his eyes blazed. "All my life I wanted to get out an extra. I never had a chance, running a small-town weekly. Now, by holy, I will."

He went off up the avenue on the dead run. Even Peter, watching him go, felt excited.

"Nice dog," he said to the hound. And the hound, at the deep gentle voice, gulped in his tongue and twitched his haunches. The whipping of his tail on the gate stone made a companionable sound for the old man. His beard folded on his chest and he nodded a little.

III

He was dozing quietly when the hound barked. It was a deep, vibrant note that anyone who knew dogs would have expected the minute he saw the spring of those ribs; it was mellow, like honey in the throat. Peter woke up tingling with the sound of it and turned to see the

hound swaying the whole hind half of himself with his tail.

Then a high loud voice shouted, "Mose, by Jeepers! What the hell you doing here, you poor dumb fool?"

Peter turned to see a stocky, short-legged man who stuck out more than was ordinary, both in front and behind. He had on a gray flannel shirt and blue denim pants, and a pair of lumberman's rubber packs on his feet, with the tops laced only to the ankle. There was a hole in the front of his felt hat where the block had worn through. He wasn't, on the whole, what you might expect to see walking on that Avenue. But Peter had seen queer people come to Heaven, and he said mildly, "Do you know this dog?"

"Sure," said the stout man. "I hunted with him round Hawkinsville for the last seven years. It's old Mose. Real smart dog. He'd hunt for anybody."

"Mose?" said Peter. "For Moses, I suppose."

"Maybe. He could track anything through hell and high water."

"Moses went through some pretty high water," said Peter. "What's your name?"

"Freem Brock. What's yours?"

Peter did not trouble to answer, for he was looking at the hound; and he was thinking he had seen some people come to Heaven's gate and look pleased, and some come and look shy, and some frightened, and some a little shame-faced, and some satisfied, and some sad (maybe with memories they couldn't leave on earth), and some jubilant, and a whole quartette still singing *Adeline* just the way they were when the hotel fell on their necks in the earthquake. But in all his career at the gate, he had never seen anyone express such pure, unstifled joy as this rawboned hound.

"Was he your dog?" he asked Freeman Brock.

"Naw," said Freem. "He belonged to Pat Haskell." He leaned his shoulder against the gatepost and crossed one foot over the other. "Stop that yawping," he said to Mose, and Mose lay down, wagging. "Maybe you ain't never been in Hawkinsville," he said to Peter. "It's a real pretty village right over the Black River. Pat kept store there and he let anybody take Mose that wanted to. Pretty often I did. He liked coming with me because I let him run foxes. I'm kind of a fox hunter," he said, blowing out his breath. "Oh, I like rabbit hunting all right, but there's no money in it . . . Say," he broke off, "you didn't tell me what your name was."

Above: *The intense, radiant eyes of this Australian shepherd cross seem to sear right through the pages of the book.* Photo © Marilyn "Angel" Wynn

Facing page: *The mighty greater Swiss mountain dog is a beautiful, bearlike dog.* Photo © Alan and Sandy Carey

"Peter," said the old man.

"Well, Pete, two years ago was Mose's best season. Seventy-seven fox was shot ahead of him. I shot thirty-seven of them myself. Five crosses and two blacks in the lot. Yes sir. I heard those black foxes had got away from the fur farm and I took Mose right over there. I made three hundred and fifty dollars out of them hides."

"He was a good dog, then?" asked Peter.

"Best foxhound in seven counties," said Freem Brock. He kicked the gate with his heel in front of Mose's nose and Mose let his ears droop. "He was a fool to hunt. I don't see no fox signs up here. Plenty rabbits in the Park. But there ain't nobody with a gun. I wish I'd brought my old Ithaca along."

"You can't kill things here," said Peter.

"That's funny. Why not?"

"They're already dead."

"Well, I know that. But it beats me how I got here. I never did nothing to get sent to this sort of place. Hell, I killed them farm foxes and I poached up the railroad in the *pre*-serve. But I never done anything bad."

"No," said St. Peter. "We know that."

"I got drunk, maybe. But there's other people done the same before me."

"Yes, Freem."

"Well, what the devil did I get sent here for, Pete?"

"Do you remember when the little girl was sick and the town doctor wouldn't come out at night on a town case, and you went over to town and made him come?"

"Said I'd knock his teeth out," said Freem, brightening.

"Yes. He came. And the girl was taken care of," said Peter.

"Aw," Freem said, "I didn't know what I was doing. I was just mad.

Well, maybe I'd had a drink, but it was a cold night, see? I didn't knock his teeth out. He left them in the glass." He looked at the old man. "Jeepers," he said. "And they sent me here for that?"

Peter looked puzzled.

"Wasn't it a good reason?" he asked. "It's not such a bad place."

"Not so bad as I thought it was going to be. But people don't want to talk to me. I tried to talk to an old timber-beast named Boone down the road. But he asked me if I ever shot a buffalo, and when I said no he went along. You're the only feller I've seen that was willing to talk to me," he said, turning to the old man. "I don't seem to miss likker up here, but there's nowhere I can get to buy some tobacco."

Two grown-up yellow Labs and a yellow Lab pup hang out in the back of a pick-up truck. Photo © William H. Mullins

The brainy border collie makes a wonderful friend for this girl. Photo © William H. Mullins

"Who loves me will love my dog also."
—St. Bernard of Clairvaux

Peter said, "You don't have to buy things in Heaven."

"Heaven?" said Freeman Brock. "Say, is that what this is?" He looked frightened all at once. "That's what the matter is. I don't belong here. I ain't the kind to come here. There must have been a mistake somewhere." He took hold of Peter's arm. "Listen," he said urgently, "do you know how to work that gate?"

"I do," said Peter. "But I can't let you out."

"I got to get out."

Peter's voice grew gentler.

"You'll like it here after a while, Freem."

"You let me out."

"You couldn't go anywhere outside," Peter said.

Freem looked through the bars at the outer heavens and watched a couple of stars, like water lilies, floating by below. He said slowly, "We'd go some place."

Peter said, "You mean you'd go out there with that dog?"

Freem flushed.

"I and Mose have had some good times," he said.

At the sound of his name, Mose's nose lifted.

Peter looked down at the ground. With the end of his shepherd's staff he thoughtfully made a cross and then another overlapping it and put an X in the upper left-hand corner. Freem looked down to see what he was doing.

"You couldn't let Mose in, could you, Pete?"

Peter sighed and rubbed out the pattern with his sandal.

"I'm sorry," he said. "The Committee don't allow dogs."

"What'll happen to the poor brute, Pete?"

Peter shook his head.

"If you ask me," Freem said loudly, "I think this is a hell of a place."

"What's that you said?"

Peter glanced up.

"Hello, Don," he said. "Meet Freem Brock. This is the editor of the paper," he said to Freem. "His name's Don."

"Hello," said Freem.

"What was that you said about Heaven being a hell of a place?" asked the editor.

Freem drew a long breath. He took a look at old Mose lying outside the gate, with his big nose resting squashed up and sideways against the bottom crossbar; he looked at the outer heavens, and he looked at the editor.

"Listen," he said. "That hound followed me up here. Pete says he can't let him in. He says I can't go out to where Mose is. I only been in jail twice," he said, "but I liked it better than this."

The editor said, "You'd go out there?"

Beagles are a breed with a long history dating back hundreds of years. They are also happy little hounds with a powerful yowl. Photo © Norvia Behling

Check out the feet on this bloodhound puppy; it is destined to be a downright big hound. Photo © Alan and Sandy Carey

"Give me the chance."

"What a story!" said the editor. "I've got my extra on the Avenue now. The cherubs will be coming this way soon. It's all about the hound, but this stuff is the genuine goods. Guest prefers to leave Heaven. Affection for old hunting dog prime factor in his decision. It's human interest. I tell you, it'll shake the Committee. By holy, I'll have an editorial in my next edition calling for a celestial referendum."

"Wait," said Peter. "What's the weather report?"

"What do you think? Fair, moderate winds, little change in temperature. But the Central Office is making up a hurricane for the South Pacific and it's due to go by pretty soon. We got to hurry, Saint."

He pounded away up the Avenue, leaving a little trail of star dust in his wake.

Freem Brock turned on Saint Peter.

"He called you something," he said.

Peter nodded.

"Saint."

"I remember about you now. Say, you're a big shot here. Why can't you let Mose in?" Peter shook his head. "I'm no big shot, Freem. If I was, maybe—"

His voice was drowned out by a shrieking up the Avenue.

"Extry! Extry! Special Edition. Read all about it. Dog outside Heaven's Gate. Dog outside . . ."

A couple of cherubs were coming down the thoroughfare, using their wings to make time. When he saw them, Freem Brock started. His shoulders began to itch self-consciously and he put a hand inside his shirt.

"My gracious," he said.

Peter, watching him, nodded.

"Everybody gets them. You'll get used to them after a while. They're handy, too, on a hot day."

"For the love of Pete," said Freem.

"Read all about it! Dog outside Heaven's Gate. Lost Dog waiting outside . . ."

"He ain't lost!" cried Freem. "He never got lost in his life."

"'Committee at fault,'" read Peter. "Thomas Aquinas isn't going to like that," he said.

"It don't prove nothing," said Freem.

"Mister, please," said a feminine voice. "The editor sent me down. Would you answer some questions?"

"Naw," said Freem, turning to look at a young woman with red hair and a gold pencil in her hand. "Well, what do you want to know, lady?"

The young woman had melting brown eyes. She looked at the hound. "Isn't he cute?" she asked. "What's his name?"

"Mose," said Freem. "He's a cute hound all right."

"Best in seven counties," said Peter.

"May I quote you on that, Saint?"

"Yes," said Peter. "You can say I think the dog ought to be let in." His face was pink over his white beard. "You can say a hurricane is going to pass, and that before I see that animal blown off by it, I'll go out there myself—I and my friend Freem. Some say I'm a has-been, but I've got some standing with the public yet."

The girl with red hair was writing furiously with a little gold glitter of her pencil. "Oh," she said.

"Say I'm going out too," said Freem. "I and Pete."

"Oh," she said. "What's your name?"

"Freeman Brock, Route 3, Boonville, New York, U. S. A."

"Thanks," she said breathlessly.

"How much longer before we got that hurricane coming?" asked Freem.

"I don't know," said the old man, anxiously. "I hope Don can work fast."

"Extry! Owner found. Saint Peter goes outside with hound, Moses. Committee bluff called. Read all about it."

"How does Don manage it so fast?" said Peter. "It's like a miracle."

"It's science," said Freem. "Hey," he yelled at a cherub.

They took the wet sheet, unheeding of the gold ink that stuck to their fingers.

"They've got your picture here, Pete."

"Have they?" Peter asked. He sounded pleased. "Let's see."

It showed Peter standing at the gate.

"It ain't bad," said Freem. He was impressed. "You really mean it?" he asked. Peter nodded.

"By cripus," Freem said slowly, "you're a pal."

Saint Peter was silent for a moment. In all the time he had minded Heaven's Gate, no man had ever called him a pal before.

On a beautiful autumn day, a girl rolls around in the cottonwood leaves with her golden pup. Photo © Henry H. Holdsworth/Wild by Nature

IV

Outside the gate, old Mose got up on his haunches. He was a weather-wise dog, and now he turned his nose outwards. The first puff of wind came like a slap in the face, pulling his ears back, and then it passed. He glanced over his shoulder and saw Freem and the old man staring at each other. Neither of them had noticed him at all. He pressed himself against the bars and lifted his nose and howled.

At his howl both men turned.

There was a clear gray point

Airedales have the goateed look of a philosophy professor. Perhaps it was an Airedale that inspired Franz Kafka to write "All knowledge, the totality of all questions and all answers, is contained in the dog." Photo © J. Faircloth/Transparencies, Inc.

Above: *With a face perhaps only a mother could love, a basset hound relaxes in the front yard*. Photo © Barbara von Hoffmann
Facing page: *Looking like a Hollywood starlet, an elegant Afghan hound poses in the humble gardens of its owner*. Photo © Tara Darling

way off along the reach of the wall, and the whine in the sky took up where Mose's howl had ended.

Peter drew in his breath.

"Come on, Freem," he said, and opened the gate. Freeman Brock hesitated. He was scared now. He could see that a real wind was coming, and the landing outside looked mighty small to him. But he was still mad, and he couldn't let an old man like Peter call his bluff.

"All right," he said. "Here goes."

He stepped out, and Mose jumped up on him, and licked his face.

"Get down, darn you," he said. "I never could break him of that trick," he explained shamefacedly to Peter. Peter smiled, closing the gate behind him with a firm hand. Its gong-like note echoed through Heaven just as the third edition burst upon the Avenue.

Freeman Brock was frightened. He glanced back through the bars, and Heaven looked good to him. Up the Avenue a crowd was gathering. A couple of lanky, brown-faced men were in front. They started toward the gate.

A black Lab on the edge of a Minnesota marsh. Photo © Bill Marchel

Then the wind took hold of him and he grasped the bars and looked outward. He could see the hurricane coming like an express train running through infinity. It had a noise like an express train. He understood suddenly just how the victim of a crossing accident must feel.

He glanced at Peter.

The old Saint was standing composedly, leaning on his staff with one hand, while with the other he drew Mose close between his legs. His white robe fluttered tight against his shanks and his beard bent sidewise like the hound's ears. He had faced lack of faith, in others: what was worse, he had faced it in himself; and a hurricane, after all, was not so much. He turned to smile at Freem. "Don't be afraid," he said.

"O.K.," said Freem, but he couldn't let go the gate.

Old Mose, shivering almost hard enough to rattle, reached up and licked Peter's hand.

One of the brown-faced men said, "That's a likely-looking hound. He the one I read about in the paper?"

"Yep," said Freem. He had to holler now.

Daniel Boone said, "Let us timber-beasts come out with you, Saint, will you?"

Peter smiled. He opened the gate with a wave of his hand, and ten or a dozen timber-beasts—Kit Carson, Jim Bridger, Nat Foster—and one of the newsboy cherubs, all crowded through and started shaking hands with him and Freeman Brock. With them was a thin, mild-eyed man.

"My name's Francis," he said to Freem when his turn came. "From Assisi."

"He's all right," Daniel Boone explained. "He wasn't much of a shot, but he knows critters. We better get holt of each other, boys."

It seemed queer to Freem. Here he was going to get blown to eternity and he didn't even know where it was, but all of a sudden he felt better than he ever had in his life. Then he felt a squirming round his legs and there was Mose, sitting on his feet, the way he would on his snowshoes in cold weather when they stopped for a sandwich on earth. He reached down and took hold of Mose's ears.

"Let her blow to blazes," he thought.

She blew.

The hurricane was on them. The nose of it went by, sweeping the wall silver. There was no more time for talk. No voices could live outside Heaven's gate. If a man had said a word, the next man to hear it would have been some poor heathen aborigine on an island in the Pacific Ocean, and he wouldn't have known what it meant.

The men on the gate stone were crammed against the bars. The wind dragged them bodily to the left, and Jim Bridger caught hold of the newsboy in the knick of time. For a minute it looked as if Jim himself was going, but they grabbed him back. There were a lot of the stoutest hands that ever swung an axe in that bunch holding onto Heaven's gate, and they weren't letting go for any hurricane—not yet.

But Freem Brock could see it couldn't last that way. He didn't care, though. He was in good company, and that was what counted the most. He wasn't a praying man, but he felt his heart swell with gratitude, and he took hold hard of the collar of Mose and felt the license riveted on. A queer thing to think of, a New York State dog license up there. He managed to look down at it, and he saw that it had turned to gold, with the collar gold under it. The wind tore at him as he saw it. The heart of the hurricane was on him now like a million devils' fingers.

"Well, Mose," he thought.

And then in the blur of his thoughts a dazzling bright light came down and he felt the gate at his back opening and he and Peter and Francis and Daniel and the boys were all drawn back into the peace of Heaven, and a quiet voice belonging to a quiet man said, "Let the dog come in."

"Jesus," said Freem Brock, fighting for breath, and the quiet man smiled, shook hands with him, and then went over and placed His arm around Peter's shoulders.

"How much is that doggie in the window? The one with the waggly tail. How much is that doggie in the window? I do hope that dog is for sale."
—Bob Merrill, How much is that doggie in the window?, *Song, 1953*

V

They were sitting together, Freem and Peter, by the gate, reading the paper in the morning warmth, and Peter was having an easy time with the editor's new type arrangement. "Gridley," he was reading the upper-case names, "Griscome, Godolphin, Habblestick, Hafey, Hanlon, Hartwell, Haskell . . ."

"Haskell," said Freem. "Not Pat?"

This Lab pup is a tad small to fit into this harness for seeing-eye dogs. Photo © Tara Darling

"Yes," said Peter. "Late of Hawkinsville."

"Not in big type?"

"Yes."

"Well, I'll be . . . Well, that twerp. Think of that. Old Pat."

Peter smiled.

"By holy," said Freem. "Ain't he going to be amazed when he finds Mose up here?"

"How's Mose doing?"

"He's all right now," said Freem. "He's been chasing the rabbits. I guess he's up there now. The dew's good."

"He didn't look so well, I thought," Peter said.

"Well, that was at first," said Freem. "You see, the rabbits just kept going up in the trees and he couldn't get a real run on any of them. There, he's got one started now."

Peter glanced up from the paper.

Old Mose was doing a slow bark, kind of low, working out the scent from the start. He picked up pace for a while, and then he seemed to strike a regular knot. His barks were deep and patient.

And then, all of a sudden, his voice broke out— that deep, ringing, honey-throated baying that Freem used to listen to in the late afternoon on the sand hills over the Black River. It went away through the public gardens and out beyond the city, the notes running together and fading and swelling and fading out.

"He's pushing him pretty fast," said Freem. "He's going to get pretty good on these rabbits."

The baying swelled again; it came back, ringing like bells. People in the gardens stopped to look up and smile. The sound of it gave Peter a warm tingling feeling.

Freem yawned.

"Might as well wait here till Pat Haskell comes in," he said.

It was pleasant by the gate, under the black and yellow parasol. It made a shade like a flower on the hot star dust. They didn't have to talk, beyond just, now and then, dropping a word between them as they sat.

After a while they heard a dog panting and saw old Mose tracking down the street. He came over to their corner and lay down at their feet, lolling a long tongue. He looked good, a little fat, but lazy and contented. After a minute, though, he got up to shift himself around, and paused as he sat down, and raised a hind leg, and scratched himself behind his wings.

Facing page: *"No one can have the part of me I give to my dogs, a gift as safe as loving a child; a part of me I guard carefully because it bears on my sanity. My dogs forgive anger in me, the arrogance in me, the brute in me. They forgive everything I do before I forgive myself."*—Guy de la Valdéne, *"For a Handful of Feathers,"* 1994. Photo © Bill Marchel

Below: *President Franklin D. Roosevelt and his beloved Scottish terrier Fala.* Photo courtesy UPI/ Corbis–Bettman

About the Editor

Todd R. Berger, a lifetime dog lover who has shared his life with too many dogs to count, is the editor of *Love of Labs, Love of Goldens, Love of German Shepherds,* and three other anthologies on outdoors subjects. He is the acquisitions editor for Voyageur Press and a freelance writer based in St. Paul, Minnesota.
Photo © Tim Berger